2062

The Gift

of the

Atonement

The *Gift*

of the

Atonement

Favorite Writings on the Atonement
and Resurrection of Jesus Christ

EAGLE
GATE

SALT LAKE CITY, UTAH

All copyrighted excerpts reproduced in this book are used by permission.

Segments from the articles "Believing Christ" by Stephen E. Robinson and "Remember How Merciful the Lord Hath Been" by W. Jeffrey Marsh, both published in the *Ensign* magazine, are © by Intellectual Reserve, Inc. Used by permission.

Original cover painting: *O My Father* © 2001 Simon Dewey

Interior art © 2001 Simon Dewey

Library of Congress Cataloging-in-Publication Data

The gift of the Atonement.
    p.   cm.
    Includes bibliographical references.
    ISBN 1-57008-780-6 (hardbound : alk. paper)
    1. Atonement.   I. Eagle Gate.

BT265.3 .G55 2002
232'.3—dc21   2001007664

Printed in the United States of America   18961-2952
R. R. Donnelley and Sons, Crawfordsville, IN

10   9   8   7   6   5

Contents

His Sacrifice in Suffering

God's Transcendent Gift

An Atonement for Sin and Death

The Breadth and Depth of the Gift

Come unto Christ

Coming to the Gift

Thanks to the following, whose efforts
helped make this book possible:

Vice-President of Publishing, Deseret Book Company
Sheri Dew

Manager of Eagle Gate Imprint, Deseret Book
Jana S. Erickson

Compiler and Editor
Jay A. Parry

Research Assistants
Dee Ann Earl Barrowes
Janna L. DeVore
Lisa Mangum
Lindsay McAllister

Art Director
Thomas E. Hewitson

Cover and Interior Art
Simon Dewey

Typographers
Tonya-Rae Facemyer
Kent R. Minson

Proofreaders
Rebecca Brady Chambers
Dayna J. Shoell

Permissions
Jan Jensen

And special thanks to the authors from many
generations whose inspired and eloquent words have
blessed us with increased understanding and gratitude for
the incomparable gift of the atonement of Jesus Christ.

Our Deepest Need

How great the importance to make these things

known unto the inhabitants of the earth, that they

may know that there is no flesh that can dwell in

the presence of God, save it be through the merits,

and mercy, and grace of the Holy Messiah.

2 NEPHI 2:8

The Means of Escape

Joseph Fielding Smith

A man walking along the road happens to fall into a pit so deep and dark that he cannot climb to the surface and regain his freedom. How can he save himself from his own folly? Not by any exertions on his own part, for there is no means of escape in the pit. He calls for help and some kindly disposed soul, hearing his cries for relief, hastens to his assistance and by lowering a ladder, gives to him the means by which he may climb again to the surface of the earth.

This was precisely the condition that Adam placed himself and his posterity in, when he partook of the forbidden fruit. All being together in the pit, none could gain the surface and relieve the others. The pit was banishment from the presence of the Lord and temporal death, the dissolution of the body. And all being subject to death, none could provide the means of escape.

Therefore, in his infinite mercy, the Father heard the cries of his children and sent his Only Begotten Son, who was not subject to death or to sin, to provide the means of escape. This he did through his infinite atonement and the everlasting gospel. . . . The Savior said, "I lay down my life for the sheep. . . . I have power to lay it down, and I have power to take it again. This commandment have I received of my Father" (John 10:15, 17–18).

Paying the Debt

Melvin J. Ballard

After the fall of Adam . . . there [was] no way nor means by which man could be raised from the grave except through the death of the Divine One. A great and eternal law had been violated, and it required the death of a God, really, to atone for the broken law and to bring to pass the salvation of man and the salvation of the world. . . .

I like to look upon it from a practical point of view, or in a way that we may clearly understand it. . . . If you had lost the home where you were born, the old family homestead that was very dear to you because in a foolish moment you overreached yourself and in excessive confidence you placed a mortgage on that home, with the thought that you could easily redeem it, would you not feel very much distressed and sad when finally it was discovered that you could not redeem it and the mortgage was to be foreclosed so that it was to pass out of your hands?

Supposing in such a moment a friend of yours could settle with the holder of that mortgage, and he would say to the holder of the mortgage, "You do not want this property."

He would say, "No, I want my money."

"Very well, I can give you the money. I will pay you. You surrender the mortgage to me."

And when that friend had paid the price and had secured the title to the homestead, would he not be a wonderful friend if he should return and say to you, "Now I know this was your home, and I know you love it. I know you are very sorry to lose it. I have redeemed it. It is mine, but I propose to give it back to you on certain conditions. They are easy. It is possible for you to fulfil them. I will not only give it back to you as it was, but I will glorify it also. I will make it more splendid and more wonderful than ever, and I will give it to you forever and ever."

Would he not be a wonderful friend? That is the kind of friend the world has in Jesus Christ. The mortgage of death was foreclosed, and death claimed its own. The grave received the body, and there it would stay forever and forever, were it not that Jesus Christ has interceded. He has settled with the holder of the mortgage. The price he paid was his life; in some way not yet perhaps fully comprehended and understood by us, he attained in that sacrifice a value of worth recognized, bartered for and exchanged and given to the holder of the mortgage, and satisfied the claims upon these earth bodies.

He has purchased us; he has redeemed us; he has bought us; and we belong to him. And now he proposed to give back these bodies glorified. To those who keep the full law he promises to give a celestial body, full of celestial power and glory and splendor; and to those who keep the terrestrial law, a body not so glorious, but still glorious and splendid; and telestial bodies to those who keep the telestial law; thus he extends to each this privilege. This is what the Lord Jesus Christ has done for man.

The Parable of the Bicycle

Stephen E. Robinson

I was sitting in a chair reading. My daughter, Sarah, who was seven years old at the time, came in and said, "Dad, can I have a bike? I'm the only kid on the block who doesn't have one."

Well, I didn't have the money then for a bike, so I stalled her. I said, "Sure, Sarah."

She said, "How? When?"

I said, "You save all your pennies, and soon you'll have enough for a bike." And she went away.

A couple of weeks later I was sitting in the same chair when I heard a "clink, clink" in Sarah's bedroom. I asked, "Sarah, what are you doing?"

She came to me with a little jar, a slit cut in the lid, and a bunch of pennies in the bottom. She said, "You promised me that if I saved all my pennies, pretty soon I'd have enough for a bike. And, Daddy, I've saved every single one of them."

My heart melted. My daughter was doing everything in her power to follow my instructions. I hadn't actually lied to her. If she saved all of her pennies, she would eventually have enough for a bike, but by then she would want a car. I said, "Let's go look at bikes."

We went to every store in town. Finally we found it— the *perfect* bicycle. She was thrilled. Then she saw the price tag, and her face fell. She started to cry. "Oh, Dad, I'll never have enough for a bicycle!"

So I said, "Sarah, how much *do* you have?"

She answered, "Sixty-one cents."

"I'll tell you what. You give me everything you've got and a hug and a kiss, and the bike is yours." Then I drove home very slowly because she insisted on riding the bike home.

As I drove beside her, I thought of the atonement of Christ. We all desperately want the celestial kingdom. We want to be with our Father in Heaven. But no matter how hard we try, we come up short. At some point all of us must realize, "I can't do this by myself. I need help." Then it is that the Savior says, in effect, "All right, you're not perfect. But what *can* you do? Give me all you have, and I'll do the rest."

He still requires our best effort. We must keep trying. But the good news is that having done all we can, it is enough. We may not be personally perfect yet, but because of our covenant with the Savior, we can rely on *his* perfection, and his perfection will get us through.

An Empty Sacrament Table

Tad R. Callister

One Sunday morning our teenaged son stood with two other priests to administer the sacrament, as they had done on many prior occasions. They pulled back the white cloth, but to their dismay there was no bread. One of them slipped out to the preparation room in hopes some could be found. There was none. Finally our troubled son made his way to the bishop and shared the concern with him. A wise bishop then stood, explained the situation to the congregation, and asked, "How would it be if the sacrament table were empty today because there were no Atonement?" I have thought of that often—what would it be like if there were no bread because there had been no crucifixion, no water because there had been no shedding of blood? If there had been no Atonement, what would the consequences be to us? Of course, the question is now moot, but it does put in perspective our total dependence on the Lord. To ask and answer this question only heightens our awareness of, and appreciation for, the Savior. What might have been, even for the "righteous," if there had been no atoning sacrifice, stirs the very depths of human emotion.

First, there would be no resurrection, or as suggested in the explicit language of Jacob: "This flesh must have laid down to rot and to crumble to its mother earth, to rise no more" (2 Nephi 9:7).

Second, our spirits would become subject to the devil. He would have "all power over you" and "seal you his"

(Alma 34:35). In fact we would become like him, even "angels to a devil" (2 Nephi 9:9).

Third, we would be "shut out from the presence of our God" (2 Nephi 9:9), to remain forever with the father of lies.

Fourth, we would "endure a never-ending torment" (Mosiah 2:39).

Fifth, we would be without hope, for "if Christ be not risen, then is our preaching vain, and your faith is also vain. . . . If in this life only we have hope in Christ, we are of all men most miserable" (1 Corinthians 15:14, 19). . . .

Without the Atonement, Macbeth's fatalistic outlook on life would have been tragically correct; it would be a play without a purpose:

> *Life's but a walking shadow, a poor player*
> *That struts and frets his hour upon the stage*
> *And then is heard no more. It is a tale*
> *Told by an idiot, full of sound and fury,*
> *Signifying nothing* (William Shakespeare, *Macbeth*, 5.5.24–28).

Life would signify nothing without Christ's redemptive act.

Our Desperate Needs

Truman G. Madsen

In the midst of our mortal predicament we have needs, even desperate needs. The first is for a mentor, an exemplar, one who has been over not just a similar road but an even far worse one. A person who can show us what we have it in us to do and to become. One who is able without hypocrisy to say to us: "What manner of men ought ye to be? Verily I say unto you even as I am" (3 Nephi 27:27).

Second, we need a person who knows the heights and depths of our frailty, our stupidities, and our failures, no matter how extreme they become. He must be no stranger to our glaring imperfections, immaturity, and rebellions. We need one who is acquainted first-hand with all these earthly weaknesses. And as a physician of mind and body, he must know the antidotes to the poisons we have inherited and imbibed.

Third, we need a person who acts in our behalf not because of compulsion nor grudgingly but because of genuine care, rooted in love—a constant and steady love. Otherwise how can we trust him? How can we be assured that at some point he will not abandon us, go his own way, let us down?

Fourth, when we run afoul of the law and founder in the aftereffects, including guilt and torment, we need, indeed we crave, an even-handed and wise judge. But we long for him to also be merciful: one who has the right, the authority, and the ability to deliver us from the threats of bondage and the compounding of our misdeeds. He must be willing, whatever the decrees of others, to use his own resources to absolve us from severe punishment, indeed, to intervene in our behalf, even if that means he himself has to pay the penalty. Most remarkable of all, he must be willing to do the same for those we have injured, mistreated, misled.

Is there any person in the universe who qualifies for such multiple roles? Only one.

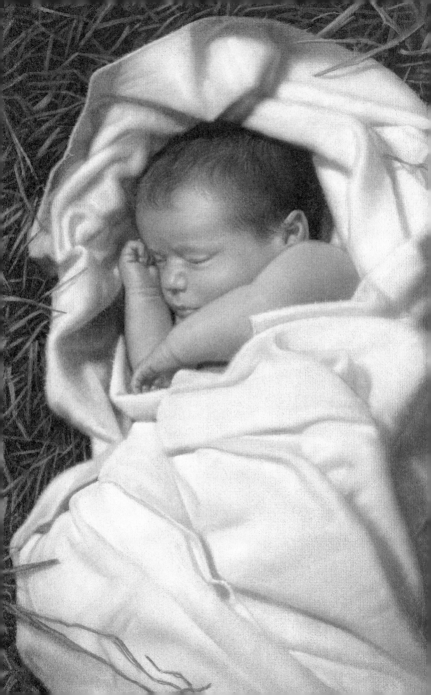

The Greatest Descent

The Son of Man hath descended below them all.

DOCTRINE AND COVENANTS 122:8

A God Is Born

Bruce R. McConkie

A God is born—how glorious is the day; how wondrous are the works which the great Creator hath wrought among us!

A God is born—angels attend; divine proclamations go forth like rolling claps of heavenly thunder; and celestial choirs sing praises to his blessed name.

A God is born—and the word is carried to the edges of eternity, that all men on all the worlds of his creating may now know that there is One who can work out the infinite and eternal atonement; there is One who can now bring to pass immortality and eternal life for all the works which his hands have made.

Well might we ask: . . . Who is he? What is the source from whence he sprang, and who are the parents who gave him life? How can a tabernacle of clay be created for the great Creator?

We answer: He is the Firstborn of the Father, the noblest and greatest spirit being of all the endless host that bear the image of the divine Elohim. He is our Elder Brother, and like us needed to gain a mortal body, to die, and to rise again in glorious immortality—all to fill the full measure of his creation.

He is the Lord Jehovah who dwelt among us as the Lord Jesus. He is the Eternal One, the Great I AM. . . . *The Only Begotten,* the Only Begotten in the flesh, the only person ever born of a mortal woman who had an immortal Father!

The Immortal God was his Father, and the mortal Mary was his mother. And it was in consequence of this birth—a birth in which mortality and immortality joined hands—that he was able to perform his atoning mission and put into operation the great and eternal plan of redemption. . . .

The scriptures say only that Joseph and Mary went to Bethlehem. . . . When they arrived all of the rooms were filled. . . . And we cannot think other than that there was a divine providence in this. The great God, the Father of us all, intended that his Only Begotten Son should be born in the lowest of circumstances and subject to the most demeaning of surroundings.

There amid the lowing of cattle and the bleating of sheep; there where the calm of the night was filled with the sounds of braying asses and yelping dogs; there where the stench of urine and the stink of dung fouled the nostrils of delicate souls—there in a stable the Son of God was born. There the King of Heaven was wrapped in swaddling clothes and laid in a manger. . . . His birth, demeaning and low and seemingly insignificant, was but a harbinger of his death. He was born in a stable and he died on a cross. . . .

We testify that a God was born some two thousand years ago and that if we follow the course he charted for us and for all men, we will have peace and joy in this life and be inheritors of eternal life in the world to come.

Divine Payment, Divine Peace

J. Reuben Clark Jr.

Forth from the infinite glory and power of the throne of God to be born to mortality in the manger-cradle in Bethlehem, came [our Lord] thenceforth to be called son of Mary, Son of man, Son of God, Jesus the Christ, the Only Begotten of the Father. God incarnate, he came not to royal courts, not to the palace of the rich, not to the home of earthly honor nor of vaunted learning of the wise and powerful, but to the humility of a lowly cottage of a village carpenter, to the home of one of us common folk.

He descended below all things that he might rise to take even captivity captive,—

"O death, where is thy sting? O grave, where is thy victory?"

Manhood found him out with the poor, the downtrodden, the oppressed, the sick, the afflicted of the earth in body and spirit, teaching his truth to their peace, their comfort, their eternal salvation and exaltation, their everlasting happiness.

The fishermen and the common folk heard, loved, and followed; the high and powerful turned their backs, scorning, deriding, reviling; they walked not after him.

He chose the foolish things to confound the wise; the weak to confound the mighty. He blessed the poor in spirit, promised comfort to them that mourn. He blessed them that hungered and thirsted for righteousness and them that are merciful. He declared the peacemakers should be called the children of God; the pure in heart should see God. He blessed the persecuted for righteousness' sake, for theirs would be the kingdom of God. He blessed the meek to inherit the earth.

He speaks to all of us who suffer for his sake, bidding us to come to him:

"Come unto me, all ye that labour and are heavy laden, and I will give you rest.

"Take my yoke upon you, and learn of me; for I am meek and lowly in heart: and ye shall find rest unto your souls.

"For my yoke is easy, and my burden is light."

So, to now and hereafter while time flows on, the Author of our being and of our salvation speaks. His words are the assurance of the lowly and humble; the hope of the mighty and great.

God help us . . . to know the divine virtue of the spiritual ointment which, to ease our wounded souls, his Son gave us as his mortality was speeding to its end. It was in the Upper Chamber the night before he poured out his life blood on the cross, so overcoming the world, an Atoning Sacrifice for the Fall of Adam and for your sins and for mine, that he bestowed this priceless heritage upon his disciples grouped around him, upon all men then and since living, and upon those hereafter to be born:

"Peace I leave with you, my peace I give unto you: not as the world giveth, give I unto you. Let not your heart be troubled, neither let it be afraid."

God grant it may so be.

The Servant King

Truman G. Madsen

His descent was a marvel of condescension, of humility, and even humiliation.

He was born in the mere outskirts of Jerusalem, in a tiny village called Bethlehem, in abject poverty.

He grew up in Nazareth, a ramshackle village of perhaps fifty families.

He went to the lowest point on earth for his baptism, in the Jordan River, which meanders to the Dead Sea, some twelve hundred feet below sea level.

A fishing village was the headquarters for his labors in Galilee.

His associates were the poor and the meek, not the prestigious officials of the Roman and Jewish hierarchies.

He knew hunger and thirst, arduous walks, and fatigue, all incurred in his efforts to reach the faltering and needy around him.

He left the Last Supper, having been totally rejected by officialdom, who were conspiring to be rid of him, and walked through the gate of garbage and refuse, leading to the city dump. As the offscouring of all things, he walked up the valley of Kidron, a deep and barren valley of tombs, to Gethsemane. . . .

He was crucified outside the city walls by the side of a road where his disgrace would be apparent to every traveler. He endured the most debasing form of torture and death: crucifixion.

While his horrified family watched from a distance, he was removed from the cross by a stranger. Then, denied the customary anointing of his body, he was dressed in the bare minimum of burial clothes and entombed.

The culmination of his descent below all things was Gethsemane and then the cross. He deliberately plunged into the consequences of the worst forms of human sin and ungodliness. Having committed no wrong and having fulfilled his mission to the letter, he yet chose to suffer as if he were guilty of the most despicable of mortal deeds. In doing so, he exposed himself to the agony of satanic buffetings. In the hardest of hard ways, these pangs descended upon him, entering his soul and enveloping him. And having "suffered for us in the flesh" (1 Peter 4:1), his bowels (in Hebrew the word translated here as *bowels* means "center self") were filled with compassion.

Because of this he knows how to succor, to heal, to comfort his people in their afflictions (see Alma 7:11). . . .

Finally, he succumbed, saying, "It is finished" (John 19:30). He had become in the complete sense, the Messiah, "the anointed one" (in Greek, *Christos*). . . . And though the world knew it not, he had now been anointed in a bloody sweat, compounded by scourging and completed by crucifixion. . . .

Within three days he emerged from the tomb, triumphant over death; his own and ours.

Son of Man, Son of God

John Taylor

As a God, He descended below all things and made Himself subject to man in man's fallen condition; as a man, He grappled with all the circumstances incident to His sufferings in the world. Anointed, indeed, with the oil of gladness above His fellows, He struggled with and overcame the powers of men and devils, of earth and hell combined; and aided by this superior power of the Godhead, He vanquished death, hell and the grave, and arose triumphant as the Son of God, the very eternal Father, the Messiah, the Prince of peace, the Redeemer, the Savior of the world; having finished and completed the work pertaining to the atonement, which His Father had given Him to do as the Son of God and the Son of man. As the Son of Man, He endured all that it was possible for flesh and blood to endure; as the Son of God, He triumphed over all, and forever ascended to the right hand of God, to further carry out the designs of Jehovah pertaining to the world and to the human family.

The Downward Journey

Tad R. Callister

The Savior's plunge into humanity was not a toe-dipping experience. It was a total immersion. He did not experience some pains and not others. His life was not a random sampling, a spot audit; it was a total confrontation with and internalization of every human experience, every human plight, every human trial. Somehow his sponge alone would absorb the entire ocean of human affliction, weakness, and suffering. For this descent he would fully bare his human breast. There would be no godly powers exercised that would shield him from one scintilla of human pain. . . .

Christ's Atonement was a descent into the seemingly "bottomless pit" of human agony. He took upon himself the sins of the most wretched of all sinners; he descended beneath the cruelest tortures devised by man. His downward journey encompassed the transgressions of those who ignorantly sinned; it incorporated that quantum of suffering unrelated to spiritual error, but nonetheless viably acute in stinging proportions—the agony of loneliness, the pain of inadequacy, the suffering of infirmities and sickness. In the course of his divine descent he was assaulted with every temptation inflicted on the human race.

After our futile attempts to explain the awesome depths of this "terrible trip," we come back again to those simple but expressive words of the scriptures, "He descended below all things" (D&C 88:6).

The How and the Why

Ezra Taft Benson

To have any measure of appreciation and gratitude for what [Jesus] accomplished in our behalf, we must remember these vital truths:

Jesus came to earth to do our Father's will.

He came with a foreknowledge that He would bear the burden of the sins of us all.

He knew he would be lifted up on the cross.

He was born to be the Savior and Redeemer of all mankind.

He was *able* to accomplish His mission because He was the Son of God and He possessed the power of God.

He was *willing* to accomplish His mission because He loves us.

No mortal being had the power or capability to redeem all other mortals from their lost and fallen condition, nor could any other voluntarily forfeit his life and thereby bring to pass a universal resurrection for all other mortals.

Only Jesus Christ was able and willing to accomplish such a redeeming act of love.

We may never understand nor comprehend in mortality *how* He accomplished what He did, but we must not fail to understand *why* He did what He did.

Everything He did was prompted by His unselfish, infinite love for us. . . .

As was so characteristic of His entire mortal experience,

the Savior submitted to our Father's will and took the bitter cup and drank.

He suffered the pains of all men in Gethsemane so they would not have to suffer if they would repent.

He submitted Himself to humiliation and insults from His enemies without complaint or retaliation.

And, finally, He endured the flogging and brutal shame of the cross. Only then did He voluntarily submit to death. In His words:

"No man taketh it [my life] from me, but I lay it down of myself. I have power to lay it down, and I have power to take it again. This commandment have I received of my Father" (John 10:18).

His Sacrifice
in Suffering

For behold, I, God, have suffered these things for all,

that they might not suffer if they would repent; . . .

which suffering caused myself, even God, the greatest

of all, to tremble because of pain, and to bleed at every

pore, and to suffer both body and spirit—and would

that I might not drink the bitter cup, and shrink—

Nevertheless, glory be to the Father, and I partook and

finished my preparations unto the children of men.

DOCTRINE AND COVENANTS 19:16–19

He Goes His Way Alone

Spencer W. Kimball

For more than three decades he lived a life of hazard and jeopardy. From Herod's horrible murder of Bethlehem's infants to Pilate's giving him to the bloodthirsty mob, Jesus was in constant danger. Perilously he lived with a price upon his head, the final price paid being thirty pieces of silver. It seemed that not only human enemies would snarl his life, but even his friends would desert him; and Satan and his cohorts would hound him ceaselessly. . . .

A price was on his head. Physical violence confronted him always. People were enjoined to reveal his whereabouts so he could be put to death. The specter of death preceded him, sat with him, walked with him, followed him. . . .

In quiet, restrained, divine dignity he stood when they cast their spittle in his face. He remained composed. Not an angry word escaped his lips. They slapped his face and beat his body. Yet he stood resolute, unintimidated. . . .

He who created the world and all that is in it, he who made the silver from which the pieces were stamped that bought him, he who could command defenders on both sides of the veil—stood and suffered.

What dignity! What mastery! What control! . . .

Yet still further tests came. Though pronounced innocent, he was scourged. Unworthy men lashed him, the pure and the Holy One, the Son of God. One word from his lips and all his enemies would have fallen to the earth, helpless.

All would have perished, all could have been as dust and ashes. Yet, in calmness, he suffered.

Even when delivered to the soldiers to be crucified, he prayed for them who despitefully used him. How he must have suffered when they violated his privacy by stripping off his clothes and then putting on him the scarlet robe! . . .

With a reed in his hand, a scarlet robe over his shoulders, and a crown of thorns on his head, he was made to suffer indignity: they laughed and mocked and jeered and challenged him. Taking the reed from his hand, they would strike him on the head. Yet he stood there, the model of long-suffering. . . .

They would have his sore and bruised and bloody body carry the cross, the weighty implement of his own death. Their strong backs unburdened, they watched him sweat and heave and strain and pull, a helpless victim. Or was he helpless? Were not the twelve legions of angels still at his command? Did they not still have their swords unsheathed? Were they not still agonizing, yet restrained from coming to the rescue? . . .

He goes his way alone. The nails are hammered into his hands and feet, through soft and quivering flesh. The agony increases. The cross is dropped in the hole; the flesh tears. What excruciating pain! Then new nails are placed in the wrist to make sure that the body will not fall to the ground and recover. . . .

His hour had come. He was alone, yet among crowds of people. Alone he was, with eager angels waiting to comfort him. Alone, with his Father in deepest sympathy but knowing that his Son must walk alone the bitter, tortuous path. Alone, drained, feverish, dying, he called out: "My God, my

God, why hast thou forsaken me?" (Matthew 27:46). Alone he had been in the garden—praying for strength to drink the bitter cup.

He had said, "Love your enemies." Now he proved how much one can love his enemies. He was dying on the cross for those who had nailed him there. As he died, he experienced agonies that no man had ever before or has since experienced. Yet he cried out, "Father, forgive them; for they know not what they do" (Luke 23:24). Was this not the last word—the supreme act? How divine to forgive those who were killing him—those who were clamoring for his blood! He had said, "Pray for them which despitefully use you," and here he was praying for them. His life met perfectly his teachings. "Be ye therefore perfect" was his command to us. With his life, his death, and his resurrection, Jesus truly has shown us the way.

Wounded, Bruised . . .

Bruce R. McConkie

Two thousand years ago, outside Jerusalem's walls, there was a pleasant garden spot, Gethsemane by name, where Jesus and his intimate friends were wont to retire for pondering and prayer. . . .

This sacred spot, like Eden where Adam dwelt, like Sinai whence Jehovah gave his laws, like Calvary where the Son of God gave his life a ransom for many, this holy ground is where the Sinless Son of the Everlasting Father took upon himself the sins of all men on condition of repentance.

We do not know, we cannot tell, no mortal mind can conceive, the full import of what Christ did in Gethsemane.

We know that he sweat great gouts of blood from every pore as he drained the dregs of that bitter cup his Father had given him.

We know that he suffered, both body and spirit, more than it is possible for man to suffer, except it be unto death.

We know that in some way, incomprehensible to us, his suffering satisfied the demands of justice, ransomed penitent souls from the pains and penalties of sin, and made mercy available to those who believe in his holy name.

We know that he lay prostrate upon the ground as the pains and agonies of an infinite burden caused him to tremble, and would that he might not drink the bitter cup.

We know that an angel came from the courts of glory to strengthen him in his ordeal. . . .

As near as we can judge, these infinite agonies—this

suffering beyond compare—continued for some three or four hours. After this, his body then wrenched and drained of strength, he confronted Judas and the other incarnate devils, some from the very Sanhedrin itself; and he was led away with a rope around his neck, as a common criminal, to be judged by the archcriminals who as Jews sat in Aaron's seat and who as Romans wielded Caesar's power.

They took him to Annas, to Caiaphas, to Pilate, to Herod, and back to Pilate. He was accused, cursed, and smitten. Their foul saliva ran down his face as vicious blows further weakened his pain-engulfed body. With reeds of wrath they rained blows upon his back. Blood ran down his face as a crown of thorns pierced his trembling brow. But above it all he was scourged, scourged with forty stripes save one, scourged with a multithonged whip into whose leather strands sharp bones and cutting metals were woven.

Many died from scourging alone, but he rose from the sufferings of the scourge that he might die an ignominious death upon the cruel cross of Calvary. Then he carried his own cross until he collapsed from the weight and pain and mounting agony of it all.

Finally, on a hill called Calvary—again, it was outside Jerusalem's walls—while helpless disciples looked on and felt the agonies of near death in their own bodies, the Roman soldiers laid him upon the cross. With great mallets they drove spikes of iron through his feet and hands and wrists. Truly he was wounded for our transgressions and bruised for our iniquities.

The Olive Press

W. Jeffrey Marsh

The lunar calendar and the Jewish calendar help us determine that there was a full moon the night Christ entered the Garden of Gethsemane. If the night was clear, Jesus would have been able to see the temple across from the garden as well as a graveyard that lay on the southern end of the Mount of Olives. After this night, the grasp of the grave over mortals would be broken. Mankind would be forever free to return to God's temple—God's presence.

Christ's suffering for the sins of the world, which allowed men to find peace with God, was performed on the Mount of Olives in an olive vineyard (Luke 22:39). The olive tree is a symbol of peace (Genesis 8:11). Olive oil provided light for lamps. Pure olive oil is a type of Christ, "the Prince of Peace" (Isaiah 9:6), the "light of the world" (John 8:12).

The word *Gethsemane* comes from the Hebrew *gath*, "press," and *shemen*, "oil." Gethsemane was a small olive grove with an olive press. Olive oil, used for healing, nutrition, light, and anointing, was extracted when the olives were subjected to immense pressure. Here, in Gethsemane, the weight of all mortal sins—past, present, and future—pressed upon the perfect, sinless Messiah and the healing "balm of Gilead" was extracted from his soul (LDS Bible Dictionary, s.v. "balm," 618). His name, Jesus the Christ, refers to his role as the Anointed One, for he was anointed before he was born to be the Redeemer of all mankind. "Jesus is spoken of as the Christ and the Messiah, which means he is the one anointed of the Father to be his personal representative in all things pertaining to the salvation of mankind. The English word *Christ* is from a Greek word meaning *anointed,* and is the equivalent of *Messiah,* which is from a Hebrew and Aramaic term meaning *anointed*" (LDS Bible Dictionary, s.v. "Anointed One," 609). His atonement empowered him to pour oil over our wounds to heal us (Luke 10:34) and give us "the oil of joy for mourning" (Isaiah 61:3).

The process for extracting oil from olives is an instructive one. Ripened olives are harvested and placed in a circular trough. A large and very heavy stone is then rolled around and around, passing over the olives to break them up. At first the olives are bruised, then they are broken, and eventually the weight of the stone turns the olives into a gray-green mash from which oozes the oil. Sometimes the mash is transferred into burlap sacks and tied off tightly. The bags are placed on a second type of press, this one having a large stone attached to a lever. The stone is lowered onto the bags of olive mash, and immense pressure is applied by turning the lever. Soon the oil begins to ooze from the olives and out through the pores of the bag. The first thing to appear is a bright red juice, which is followed by the clear-colored olive oil.

In Gethsemane, this place of pressing, Jesus was pressed down by the weight of the sins and suffering of the world until his atoning blood, which provides us with healing, oozed from every pore (Matthew 26:36–37; Luke 22:44; D&C 19:18). "Surely he hath borne our griefs, and carried our sorrows. . . . He was wounded for our transgressions, he was bruised for our iniquities" (Isaiah 53:4–5). The olive trees in the Garden of Gethsemane today are gnarled and twisted, as if bearing witness of the agony that took place there for us.

A Vision of Gethsemane

Orson F. Whitney

I seemed to be in the Garden of Gethsemane, a witness of the Savior's agony. I saw Him as plainly as ever I have seen anyone. Standing behind a tree in the foreground, I beheld Jesus, with Peter, James and John, as they came through a little wicket gate at my right. Leaving the three apostles there, after telling them to kneel and pray the Son of God passed over to the other side, where He also knelt and prayed. It was the same prayer with which all Bible readers are familiar; "Oh my Father, if it be possible let this cup pass from me; nevertheless not as I will, but as thou wilt."

As He prayed the tears streamed down His face, which was toward me. I was so moved at the sight that I also wept, out of pure sympathy. My whole heart went out to Him; I loved Him with all my soul, and longed to be with Him as I longed for nothing else.

Presently He arose and walked to where those apostles were kneeling—fast asleep! He shook them gently, awakened them, and in a tone of tender reproach, untinctured by the least show of anger or impatience, asked them plaintively if they could not watch with Him one hour. There He was, with the awful weight of the world's sin upon His shoulders, with the pangs of every man, woman and child shooting through His sensitive soul—and they could not watch with Him one poor hour!

Returning to His place, He offered up the same prayer as before; then went back and again found them sleeping.

Again He awoke them, readmonished them, and once more returned and prayed. Three times this occurred until I was perfectly familiar with His appearance—face, form and movements. He was of noble stature and majestic mien—not at all the weak, effeminate being that some painters have portrayed; but the very God that He was and is, as meek and humble as a little child.

All at once the circumstances seemed to change, the scene remaining just the same. Instead of before, it was after the crucifixion, and the Savior, with the three apostles, now stood together in a group at my left. They were about to depart and ascend into Heaven. I could endure it no longer. I ran from behind the tree, fell at His feet, clasped Him around the knees and begged Him to take me with Him.

I shall never forget the kind and gentle manner in which He stooped, raised me up, and embraced me. It was so vivid! So real! I felt the very warmth of His body, as He held me in His arms and said in tenderest tones; "No, my son; these have finished their work: they can go with me, but you must stay and finish yours." Still I clung to Him. Gazing up into His face—for he was taller than I—I besought Him fervently; "Well, promise me that I will come to you at the last." Smiling sweetly, He said: *"That will depend entirely upon yourself."* I awoke with a sob in my throat, and it was morning.

"And It Was Night"

Truman G. Madsen

May I offer a glimpse of what must have gone through Him and of what He must have gone through. "Mine hour," He had said often, "has not yet come," but now it had. After the Last Supper the record says, "and it was night" (John 13:30). . . .

Somewhere, somewhere on that mountain, He knelt.

I have witnessed the effort of the most pious of Jews as they stand—they do not kneel—at the place that is but a remnant of the wall below the ancient walls of the temple mount. Rhythmically, they throw their whole bodies into their prayer. They are sometimes ridiculed for this. They say: "We are fighting distraction. We want to concentrate. Movement helps." Well, the movement of that night, I suggest, was internal, not external, and somehow the bitterness was as bitter as gall. . . .

That burden, that bitterness, He vicariously took within. "How?" we cry out. But a child can understand. Pain hurts. Even the presence of it hurts those of us who merely stand detached and observe. The Savior, who is supersensitive and did not take a backward step from the will of the Father, could and did feel for and with us. The pressure worked upon Him. Somewhere on the road between the north and the south, He cried out, anticipating, "Father, save me from this hour." We don't know how long was the interim between that sentence and prayer and the next, but He then cried: "But for this cause came I unto this hour. Father, glorify thy name." And the voice said, "I have both glorified it, and will glorify it again" (John 12:27–28).

Luke, who tradition says was a physician, recorded that great drops of blood came from the Savior's pores (Luke 22:44). The bitterness oozed. It is not a spectacle one wishes to recall, but we have been commanded, and weekly we memorialize it in an ordinance called the sacrament. Even then, all His preparation and all that He could summon from His own strength was not sufficient. And more earnestly, says the record, He prayed, and an angel came, strengthening Him (see Luke 22:43–44). Strengthening, but not delivering. What is it like to have the power to summon legions of angels to end the ordeal yet not to summon them? During that same night He was betrayed. He was taken prisoner. He was broken into, pierced by scourging; and a merciful reading of Pilate's motives suggests that he hoped this would suffice for those who were crying out against Jesus. It did not. The weight, I submit, had begun there on the mount, a much greater weight than the weight of the cross that He was then to bear.

Now, what conclusions can we draw from all this? First, hereafter when we speak or hear the words, "I anoint you with this consecrated oil," let us remember what the consecration cost.

As we sit—but in our spirits as we kneel during the sacrament service—and are asked to remember His body, recall that it was the veritable tree and olive beaten for the light, and that there flows from that mount unto this whole earth, and beyond, the redemptive power of healing and soothing and ministering to the needy.

In the hours of gladness, should our cup run o'er, let us

remember that to make that possible, a cup—the bitterest of cups—must have been drunk.

On that day when our life, the life of attempted faithfulness, is bludgeoned and becomes wearing and wearying, may we remember that no great and good fruits come easily, that we are the olive plants who were supposedly planted anew in Him, and that only time and suffering and endurance can produce the peaceable fruit which He yearns for us to have. He does not deliver until the perfect work has done its work. . . . He pleads even now for more time, for you and for me, until we too have been purged and can sing the song of redeeming love.

The Supreme Prayer

Bruce R. McConkie

Of all the prayers ever uttered, in time or in eternity—by gods, angels, or mortal men—this one stands supreme, above and apart, preeminent over all others.

In this garden called Gethsemane, . . . the greatest member of Adam's race, the One whose every thought and word were perfect, pled with his Father to come off triumphant in the most torturous ordeal ever imposed on man or God.

There, amid the olive trees—in the spirit of pure worship and perfect prayer—Mary's Son struggled under the most crushing burden ever born by mortal man.

There, . . . while Peter, James, and John slept—with prayer on his lips—God's own Son took upon himself the sins of all men on conditions of repentance.

Upon his Suffering Servant, the great Elohim, there and then, placed the weight of all the sins of all men of all ages who believe in Christ and seek his face. And the Son, who bore the image of the Father, pled with his divine Progenitor for power to fulfill the chief purpose for which he had come to earth.

This was the hour when all eternity hung in the balance. So great was the sin-created agony—laid on him who knew no sin—that he sweat great drops of blood from every pore, and "would," within himself, that he "might not drink the bitter cup" (D&C 19:18). From creation's dawn to this supreme hour, and from this atoning night through all the endless ages of eternity, there neither had been nor would be again such a struggle as this.

A Cry from the Heart

John Taylor

Jesus had to take away sin by the sacrifice of Himself, the just for the unjust. . . . And as He in His own person bore the sins of all, and atoned for them by the sacrifice of Himself, so there came upon Him the weight and agony of ages and generations, the indescribable agony consequent upon this great sacrificial atonement wherein He bore the sins of the world. . . . Hence His profound grief, His indescribable anguish, His overpowering torture, all experienced in the submission to the eternal fiat of Jehovah and the requirements of an inexorable law.

. . . In making an atonement for the sins of the world He bore the weight, the responsibility, and the burden of the sins of all men, which, to us, is incomprehensible. As stated, "the Lord, your Redeemer, suffered death in the flesh; wherefore he suffereth the pains of all men;" and Isaiah says: "Surely he hath borne our griefs and carried our sorrows," also, "The Lord hath laid on him the iniquity of us all," . . . or, as it is written in the Second Book of Nephi: "For behold, he suffereth the pains of all men; yea, the pains of every living creature, both men, women and children, who belong to the family of Adam." . . .

Groaning beneath this concentrated load, this intense, incomprehensible pressure, this terrible exaction of Divine justice, from which feeble humanity shrank, and through the agony thus experienced sweating great drops of blood, He was led to exclaim, "Father, if it be possible, let this cup pass from me." He had wrestled with the superincumbent load in the wilderness, He had struggled against the powers of darkness that had been let loose upon Him there; placed below all things, His mind surcharged with agony and pain, lonely and apparently helpless and forsaken, in His agony the blood oozed from His pores. Thus rejected by His own, attacked by the powers of darkness, and seemingly forsaken by His God, on the cross He bowed beneath the accumulated load, and cried out in anguish, "My God, my God, why hast thou forsaken me!"

The Statistics of Sin

Gerald N. Lund

In all the world, there was only one perfectly holy, perfectly sinless being (see Hebrews 4:15; D&C 20:22). Only one man lived his very life without a single thought, word, or action that was out of harmony with the will of God. And yet, so that he could bring about our redemption, he stood before the justice of God and paid as though he were guilty of every sin and every transgression ever committed. We cannot begin to quantify or comprehend the vastness of the requirements of that suffering.

Yet, to help us begin to grasp with our finite, mortal minds the enormous price required, consider a few rough indicators of how much sin there is in our world. If you look at the United States alone, there are now more than fifty murders committed every day (that's nearly 19,000 per year). There are more than 21,000 thefts reported every day, and more than 5,500 reported cases of child neglect and abuse. (All figures are based on 1987 or 1988 statistics for the United States only. See *1991 Information Please Almanac*, New York, 1991, 3.) Alma said adultery is the second most serious sin next to murder (see Alma 39:5). Think of how many times in a single day adultery or some other violation of the law of chastity is committed somewhere in the world. How many cases of incest, child abuse, pornography, burglary, robbery? How many times in any one day is the name of God taken in vain? How many times are sacred things profaned? Then multiply these over the span of human history. And that takes into consideration only our world. We know that the Atonement extended to other worlds as well. . . .

Jesus went to the Garden and to the cross and paid in personal suffering an infinite price for all of these horrible, unthinkable things. That gives a completely different meaning to the command, "Behold the condescension of God!"

. . . [And] he chose to suffer not only for our sins but for the infirmities, sicknesses, and illnesses of mankind. . . .

Who could even begin to fathom the depths of the suffering and the depths of the pain that the Savior condescended to take upon himself so that he could meet the needs of his children and redeem them? No wonder it could be said, "The Son of Man hath descended below them all" (D&C 122:8).

"An Incomprehensible Tidal Wave"

Tad R. Callister

Elder Marion G. Romney [taught]: "Jesus then went into the Garden of Gethsemane. There he suffered most. He suffered greatly on the cross, of course, but other men had died by crucifixion. . . . But no man, nor set of men, *nor all men put together, ever suffered what the Redeemer suffered in the garden*" (Conference Report, October 1953, 35; emphasis added).

What a doctrine! The composite suffering of all men, of all ages, of all worlds does not surpass the Savior's suffering in the Garden. How can we begin to comprehend the cumulative suffering of all mankind, or as taught by Elder Orson F. Whitney, "the piled up agony of the human race" (*Saturday Night Thoughts*, Salt Lake City, 1921, 152)? What is thrown on the scale of remorse, as observed by Truman Madsen, when we aggregate "the cumulative impact of our vicious thoughts, motives, and acts" (*Christ and the Inner Life*, Salt Lake City, 1988, 4)? What, as Elder Vaughn J. Featherstone inquired, is the "weight and immensity of the penalties of all broken laws crying from the dust and from the future—an incomprehensible tidal wave of guilt" (*The Disciple of Christ*, Salt Lake City, 1984, 4)? How many searing consciences has this world produced and to what depths of depravity has this earthly sphere sunk? Can anyone possibly fathom the horrendous consequences of such sin? Not only did the Savior fathom it—he felt it, and he suffered it.

Crossing the Line to Infinite

Stephen E. Robinson

The suffering of Jesus Christ in the Garden and on the cross exceeded the combined suffering of all human beings. The suffering of Jesus was not just tough pain and a bad death, it was not just the most painful of all human experiences and deaths. The suffering of Christ was cumulative; it was in fact infinite. When Christ descended below all things, he crossed the line from the finite, that which can be measured, to the infinite. And as his suffering was infinite, so now is his glory infinite, and infinite also is his power to save. . . . "Therefore there can be nothing which is short of an infinite atonement which will suffice for the sins of the world" (Alma 34:12; see also 2 Nephi 25:16; Alma 34:10, 14; D&C 19:10–19).

Human nature makes us want to quantify, to measure the atonement of Christ, but his ordeal is off any scale; it is beyond our comprehension. Jesus bore not just the sins of the world, but the sorrows, pains, and sicknesses of the world as well . . . (see Alma 7:11–12). . . .

All the negative aspects of human existence brought about by the Fall, Jesus Christ absorbed into himself. He experienced vicariously in Gethsemane all the private griefs and heartaches, all the physical pains and handicaps, all the emotional burdens and depressions of the human family. He knows the loneliness of those who don't fit in or who aren't handsome or pretty. He knows what it's like to choose up teams and be the last one chosen. He knows the anguish of parents whose children go wrong. He knows the private hell of the abused child or spouse. He knows all these things personally and intimately because he lived them in the Gethsemane experience. Having personally lived a perfect life, he then chose to experience our imperfect lives. In that infinite Gethsemane experience, the meridian of time, the center of eternity, he lived a billion billion lifetimes of sin, pain, disease, and sorrow.

God uses no magic wand to simply wave bad things into nonexistence. The sins that he remits, he remits by making them his own and suffering them. The pain and heartaches that he relieves, he relieves by suffering them himself. These things can be shared and absorbed, but they cannot be simply wished or waved away. They must be suffered. Thus we owe him not only for our spiritual cleansing from sin, but for our physical, mental, and emotional healings as well, for he has borne these infirmities for us also. All that the Fall put wrong, the Savior in his atonement puts right. It is all part of his infinite sacrifice—of his infinite gift.

Victorious Christ

James E. Talmage

Christ's agony in the garden is unfathomable by the finite mind, both as to intensity and cause. . . . He struggled and groaned under a burden such as no other being who has lived on earth might even conceive as possible. It was not physical pain, nor mental anguish alone, that caused Him to suffer such torture as to produce an extrusion of blood from every pore; but a spiritual agony of soul such as only God was capable of experiencing. No other man, however great his powers of physical or mental endurance, could have suffered so. . . . In that hour of anguish Christ met and overcame all the horrors that Satan, "the prince of this world" (John 14:30) could inflict. . . .

In some manner, actual and terribly real though to man incomprehensible, the Savior took upon Himself the burden of the sins of mankind from Adam to the end of the world. . . .

From the terrible conflict in Gethsemane, Christ emerged a victor. Though in the dark tribulation of that fearful hour He had pleaded that the bitter cup be removed from His lips, the request, however oft repeated, was always conditional; the accomplishment of the Father's will was never lost sight of as the object of the Son's supreme desire. The further tragedy of the night, and the cruel inflictions that awaited Him on the morrow, to culminate in the frightful tortures of the cross, could not exceed the bitter anguish through which He had successfully passed.

The Rescue Mission

Tad R. Callister

The Savior's sacrifice required inexhaustible stamina in order to bear the consequences of our sins and weather the temptations of the Evil One. But his suffering must have been more than a resigned submissiveness or a fist-clenching "taking of the stripes." It must have been more than a defensive "holding of the fort" or raising of the shield to ward off the fiery darts of the Evil One. Part of the Savior's atoning quest must have included an element of conquering, an offensive struggle of sorts. . . .

With merciless fury Satan's forces must have attacked the Savior on all fronts—frantically, diabolically, seeking a vulnerable spot, a weakness, an Achilles' heel through which they might inflict a "mortal" wound, all in hopes they could halt the impending charge, but it was not to be. The Savior pressed forward in bold assault until every prisoner was freed from the tenacious tentacles of the Evil One. This was a rescue mission of infinite implications. Every muscle of the Savior, every virtue, every spiritual reservoir that could be called upon would be summoned in the struggle. No doubt there was an exhaustion of all energies, a straining of all faculties, an exercise of all powers. Only then, when seemingly all had been spent, would the forces of evil abandon their posts and retreat in horrible defeat. . . . The Great Deliverer has rescued us—saved the day, saved eternity. But, oh, what a battle! What wounds! What love! What cost!

No Spot of Weakness

Gerald N. Lund

We have been told many times that there is, in the life of Jesus, a model to which we can turn as we seek to mold and sculpt our own lives into works of perfection. It matters not at which point we focus the eye of scrutiny. Examine the life of Christ as minutely as you wish. No hint of blemished conduct, no trace of lost control, no moment of foolish passion, no spot of crumbling weakness can be found. Jesus is the perfect man. Every moment of his recorded life inspires those who would bring themselves to that level of perfection marked out in the indelible chalk of Christ's own life.

In the trial, arrest, and execution of Jesus we find no exception to this unmatched faultlessness. In those hours of life when he was being ground with merciless pressure, his balance was never threatened, his composure never marred. The betrayal of Judas, the denial of Peter, the gross injustice of his trial, the savagery of the mob, the cowardice of Pilate, even the weeping of his mother at the foot of the cross—nothing could loosen his hold on perfect control; nothing could lessen his total mastery. Christ's marvelous ability to face adversity without loss of balance or faith in God is one of the great lessons we can learn from him.

In addition, he taught by his own example that God's will takes priority over all. Submission to the Father is paramount even if it means pain, ridicule, and death. Obedience must remain firm under all conditions, even unto death, if one is to be found worthy of him (D&C 98:14–15). Here again, the Son set the perfect example for us. Torture, injustice, the supreme irony of being condemned for blasphemy, the agony in the garden, the sadistically cruel death by crucifixion—all of these combined could not divert him from his determination to do the will of the Father.

Sometimes when circumstances corner a man and leave him no alternative, he may show great courage and strength of will. However, Christ showed those qualities throughout, even though he could have escaped at any moment. The powers of heaven, we are told, are controlled by righteousness (see D&C 121:36). Keeping in mind that his was a perfectly sinless life, fathom, if you can, the powers Jesus had at his command. How pitifully futile the might of Pilate's Roman garrison would have been in the face of the twelve heavenly legions Christ could have summoned, but didn't (see Matthew 26:53). How easy it would have been for the one who cast out devils to banish the arrogant high priest. How elementary for one who loosed the tongues of the dumb to stop the tongues of false witnesses. Yet he who brought worlds and galaxies into being stood mute before his mortal accusers. He who stilled the rushing winds and pounding waves of the Sea of Galilee stilled not the stormy cries of "Crucify him! Crucify him!" He who had escaped unharmed from the angry mob at Nazareth (see Luke 4:29–30) faced the small band of arresting soldiers with a simple "I am he" (see John 18:5). The awesome, infinite power at his command was not unleashed to spare himself the least pain, the smallest discomfort. His will was irrevocably interwoven with that of the Father's, and nothing deterred him from its accomplishment.

God's Transcendent Gift

The wages of sin is death; but the gift of God is

eternal life through Jesus Christ our Lord.

ROMANS 6:23

The Cost

Melvin J. Ballard

I think as I read the story of Abraham's sacrifice of his son Isaac that our Father is trying to tell us what it cost him to give his Son as a gift to the world. You remember the story of how Abraham's son came after long years of waiting and was looked upon by his worthy sire, Abraham, as more precious than all his other possessions; yet, in the midst of his rejoicing, Abraham was told to take this only son and offer him as a sacrifice to the Lord. He responded. Can you feel what was in the heart of Abraham on that occasion? . . . What do you think was in his heart when he started away from Mother Sarah, and they bade her goodbye? . . . I imagine it was about all Father Abraham could do to keep from showing his great grief and sorrow at that parting, but he and his son trudged along three days toward the appointed place, Isaac carrying the fagots that were to consume the sacrifice. The two travelers rested, finally, at the mountainside, and the men who had accompanied them were told to remain while Abraham and his son started up the hill.

The boy then said to his father: "Why, Father, . . . we have the fire to burn the sacrifice; but where is the sacrifice?"

It must have pierced the heart of Father Abraham to hear the trusting and confiding son say: "You have forgotten the sacrifice." Looking at the youth, his son of promise, the poor father could only say: "The Lord will provide."

They ascended the mountain, gathered the stones together, and placed the fagots upon them. Then Isaac was bound, hand and foot, kneeling upon the altar. I presume Abraham, like a true father, must have given his son his farewell kiss, his blessing, his love, and his soul must have been drawn out in that hour of agony toward his son who was to die by the hand of his own father. Every step proceeded until the cold steel was drawn, and the hand raised that was to strike the blow to let out the life's blood when the angel of the Lord said: "It is enough."

Our Father in heaven went through all that and more, for in his case the hand was not stayed. He loved his Son, Jesus Christ, better than Abraham ever loved Isaac, . . . and yet he allowed this well-beloved Son to descend from his place of glory and honor, where millions did him homage, down to the earth, a condescension that is not within the power of man to conceive. He came to receive the insult, the abuse, and the crown of thorns. God heard the cry of his Son in that moment of great grief and agony, in the garden when, it is said, the pores of his body opened and drops of blood stood upon him, and he cried out: "Father, if thou be willing, remove this cup from me."

I ask you, what father and mother could stand by and listen to the cry of their children in distress, in this world, and not render aid and assistance? I have heard of mothers throwing themselves into raging streams when they could not swim a stroke to save their drowning children, rushing into burning buildings to rescue those whom they loved.

We cannot stand by and listen to those cries without its touching our hearts. The Lord has not given us the power to save our own. He has given us faith, and we submit to the inevitable, but he had the power to save, and he loved his Son, and he could have saved him. He might have rescued him from the insult of the crowds. He might have rescued him when the crown of thorns was placed upon his head. He might have rescued him when the Son, hanging between the two thieves, was mocked with, "Save thyself, and come down from the cross. He saved others; himself he cannot save." He listened to all this. He saw that Son condemned; he saw him drag the cross through the streets of Jerusalem and faint under its load. He saw that Son finally upon Calvary; he saw his body stretched out upon the wooden cross; he saw the cruel nails driven through hands and feet, and the blows that broke the skin, tore the flesh, and let out the life's blood of his Son. He looked upon that.

In the case of our Father, the knife was not stayed, but it fell, and the life's blood of his Beloved Son went out. His Father looked on with great grief and agony over his Beloved Son, until there seems to have come a moment when even our Savior cried out in despair: "My God, my God, why hast thou forsaken me?"

In that hour I think I can see our dear Father behind the veil looking upon these dying struggles until even he could not endure it any longer; and, like the mother who bids farewell to her dying child, has to be taken out of the room, so as not to look upon the last struggles, so he bowed his head, and hid in some part of his universe, his great heart almost breaking for the love that he had for his Son. Oh, in that moment when he might have saved his Son, I thank him and praise him that he did not fail us, for he had not only the love of his Son in mind, but he also had love for us. I rejoice that he did not interfere, and that his love for us made it possible for him to endure to look upon the sufferings of his Son and give him finally to us, our Savior and our Redeemer.

Merciful Love

Gerald N. Lund

The Savior . . . owed no debt to the law, but he went before it and in essence said: "I am perfect and therefore owe you no suffering. However, I will pay the debt for all mankind. I will undergo suffering that I might pay the price for every transgression and sin ever committed by any man."

And so, in the Garden of Gethsemane, Christ stood before the law and paid the price in suffering for every sin as though he himself had committed them. Such suffering was beyond the power of any mortal man to endure. We can't understand how he did it, only that he did, and that "through Him mercy can be fully extended to each of us without offending the eternal law of justice" (Boyd K. Packer, *Ensign*, May 1977, 56). In terms of [a well-known] parable, he generated sufficient payment to satisfy the debt of every other man. He met the demands of the law for himself through obedience, and for all others through suffering.

Alma told his son Corianton that mercy could not rob justice, or else "God would cease to be God" (Alma 42:25). And the merciful love of the Father and the Son did not rob justice of its rightful demands. Rather, it paid justice! Their Love said to Justice, by virtue of the price paid in the Garden, "Here is payment for the wrongs committed. You are paid in full. Now let the captives go free."

In one of the most beautiful images in all of scripture, we find the solution to that awful dilemma we all face as sinners. We are standing before the bar as defendants, facing the great judge, God the Father. Our defense attorney—our "Advocate with the Father"—steps forward, not to refute the charges or to hold up a record of good works on our part to counterbalance our guilt, but to plead our case in a different manner:

"Listen to him who is the advocate with the Father, who is pleading your cause before him—

"Saying: Father, behold the sufferings and death of him who did no sin, in whom thou wast well pleased; behold the blood of thy Son which was shed, the blood of him whom thou gavest that thyself might be glorified;

"Wherefore, Father, spare these my brethren that believe on my name, that they may come unto me and have everlasting life" (D&C 45:3–5).

Nothing man could do for himself could bring him past that judgment bar successfully without such an Advocate. That is why eternal life is always a gift, and those who receive it do so by "inheritance." It is interesting to note that the word *inherit* and its cognate words are used seventy-eight times in the Doctrine and Covenants, while the word *earned* and its related words are not used once.

One of the Grand Constants in Nature

Hugh Nibley

In its sweep and scope, atonement takes on the aspect of one of the grand constants in nature—omnipresent, unalterable, such as gravity or the speed of light. Like them it is always there, easily ignored, hard to explain, and hard to believe in without an explanation. Also, we are constantly exposed to its effects whether we are aware of them or not. Alma found that it engages the mind like a physical force, focusing thought with the intensity of a laser beam (see Alma 36:17–19). Like gravity, though we are rarely aware of it, it is at work every moment of our lives, and to ignore it can be fatal. It is waiting at our disposal to draw us on.

Once or Twice in a Thousand Years

Bruce R. McConkie

Once or twice in a thousand years—perhaps a dozen times since mortal man became of dust a living soul—an event of such transcendent import occurs that neither heaven nor earth are ever thereafter the same.

Once or twice in a score of generations the hand from heaven clasps the hand on earth in perfect fellowship, the divine drama unfolds, and the whole course of mortal events changes.

Now and then in a quiet garden, or amid the fires and thunders of Sinai, or inside a sepulchre that cannot be sealed, or in an upper room—almost always apart from the gaze of men and seldom known by more than a handful of people—the Lord intervenes in the affairs of men and manifests his will relative to their salvation. . . .

The most transcendent of all such events occurred in a garden called Gethsemane, outside Jerusalem's walls, when the Chief Citizen of planet earth sweat great drops of blood from every pore as he in agony took upon himself the sins of all men on conditions of repentance. Yet another of these events, destined to affect the life and being of every living soul, happened in the Arimathean's tomb when the sinless spirit of the one perfect man returned from the paradise of God to inhabit again—this time in glorious immortality—the pierced and slain body that once was his.

The Very Heart

George W. Pace

The atonement of Christ is the most important event that has transpired or ever will transpire among all of God's creations. It is the very source of all life, light, power, truth, and love, and the center and object of all redemptive faith. . . .

In other words, the Atonement is the very heart of the gospel of Jesus Christ. Even as the human heart pumps life-giving blood to all parts of the body, so will the Atonement, if understood properly, act as a great spiritual heart, pumping life-giving blood through the ordinances and principles of the gospel to the life and soul of every member of the Church. Is it any wonder that every ordinance and principle . . . is given from God to man to typify, or foreshadow, the Savior and his atonement? . . .

Even though the Atonement was wrought nearly two thousand years ago, its reality to us and its effect on us can be as great as though we had been contemporaries of the Savior living in Jerusalem. Indeed, under the quiet workings of the Holy Ghost, we can stand, as it were, in the Garden of Gethsemane, as witness of the Savior's agony; we can stand, as it were, at the foot of Golgotha and obtain an overwhelming awareness of the pain of the cross; we can receive in our hearts a measure, and only as the Spirit can reveal it, of the tremendous pain, sorrow, and humiliation he suffered. We can, in other words, experience in part the majesty of the Atonement and make it the greatest event in our lives.

The Work of a God

Robert L. Millet

To Christ we turn in the hour of need; he is the balm of Gilead. Upon him and his word we may rely with unshaken confidence; he is true and faithful. From him we can receive the realization of our fondest dreams; his name is Eternal, and the life we may enjoy with him is called Eternal Life.

To have faith in the name of Christ is to have an assurance, born of the Spirit, of our Lord's divine sonship, to know by revelation that no earthly man or woman—no matter how gifted and no matter how noble—could have done what he did. His work was and is the work of a God, and the product of his labors—salvation itself—is available only because of the merciful intercession of one with power over life and death.

To have faith in the name of Christ is to acknowledge his hand in all things, to confess that there are labors beyond the power of man to perform. Man cannot forgive his own sins any more than he can create himself. Man cannot cleanse and renew and regenerate the human soul any more than he can resurrect himself. These are the infinite actions of a God, and they require the intervention of godly powers in man's behalf. To have faith in the name of Christ is to recognize and receive the saving grace of Christ.

The power unto life and salvation is in Jesus Christ, the person. The power is not in programs, even inspired programs. Programs cannot save. They have not the power to forgive sins or sanctify or soothe troubled souls. It is the gospel of

Jesus Christ that is "the power of God unto salvation" (Romans 1:16), a power that derives from him who is omnipotent. The Saints of all ages come to know by revelation the source of their salvation. Christianity without the living Christ is at best deficient. Righteousness without the Righteous One cannot redeem. Theology without the gospel lacks the power of salvation.

This I Know

Bruce R. McConkie

Creation is father to the Fall; and by the Fall came mortality and death; and by Christ came immortality and eternal life. If there had been no fall of Adam, by which cometh death, there could have been no atonement of Christ, by which cometh life.

And now, as pertaining to this perfect atonement, wrought by the shedding of the blood of God, I testify that it took place in Gethsemane and at Golgotha; and as pertaining to Jesus Christ, I testify that he is the son of the Living God and was crucified for the sins of the world. He is our Lord, our God, and our King. This I know of myself, independent of any other person. I am one of his witnesses, and in a coming day I shall feel the nail marks in his hands and in his feet and shall wet his feet with my tears. But I shall not know any better then than I know now that he is God's Almighty Son, that he is our Savior and Redeemer, and that salvation comes in and through his atoning blood and in no other way.

God grant that all of us may walk in the light as God our Father is in the light so that, according to the promises, the blood of Jesus Christ his Son will cleanse us from all sin.

An Atonement for Sin and Death

O how great the goodness of our God, who prepareth a

way for our escape from the grasp of this awful monster;

yea, that monster, death and hell, which I call the

death of the body, and also the death of the spirit.

2 NEPHI 9:10

Spiritual Estrangement

Brent L. Top

President Harold B. Lee once stated, "The heaviest burden that anyone can carry in life is the burden of sin." Each of us has borne and continues to bear that burden to some degree or another. . . .

. . . Who among us has not felt the fear that comes from acknowledging the justice of God's pronouncements and indictments against our evil ways? Who among us has not tasted the bitterness of that cup? Who among us has not felt the spiritual and emotional turmoil of the soul, like unto a "troubled sea" that "cannot rest"? Who among us has not experienced feelings similar to those described in the Book of Mormon by Alma?

"But I was racked with eternal torment, for my soul was harrowed up to the greatest degree and racked with all my sins . . ." (Alma 36:12). . . .

The burden of sin also creates a feeling of worthlessness as well as unworthiness. It often makes us feel that we can do nothing right. Our sense of shame falsely makes us feel that we are unworthy to approach our Father in Heaven in worship or in prayer. This further estranges us from our most important advocate and ally. "There is no loneliness so great, so absolute, so utterly complete," wrote Elder Richard L. Evans, "as the loneliness of a man who cannot call upon his God" (*Richard Evans' Quote Book*, Salt Lake City, 1971, 148).

Sinning brings a sense of loneliness even when we are surrounded by others. . . . The Spirit of the Lord is grieved and withdrawn, and we are left alone—without the comfort, enlightenment, and inspiration of the Holy Ghost. There is no greater emptiness than to be void of the Spirit of the Lord. . . .

All too often accompanying our sin-induced spiritual sickness is the added discomfort of deception—of hiding a "dark secret." Many of us have felt that sense of hypocrisy that comes from knowing that our life does not reflect our professed ideals. One student who had cheated on a test in school described an audible voice speaking to his soul each time he attempted to pray or bless the sacrament. It whispered, "You're a liar! You're a cheat! You're a hypocrite!" . . .

When we are weighted down with the burdens of sin, our souls are truly like the river of filthy waters (see 1 Nephi 15:26–30), made turbulent by the constant churning of guilt and shame. It seems as though there is no relief from the despair and the discouragement and the horror of hypocrisy. Even Alma's graphic description of his agony does not fully capture the unquenchable emotional, spiritual, and mental "fire" that burns within a sinner's soul. . . .

. . . From our own suffering and sorrow for sin come such soul-searching questions as "What if this burden of sin and shame can never be lifted?" and "What if I must feel 'eternal torment' and the 'pains of hell' forever?" Surely such thoughts strike within us a feeling described by Alma as "inexpressible horror."

Such would have been the case without the loving intercession of our Savior, Jesus Christ. Without the "infinite atonement," not only would we suffer the pains of hell and carry the burdens of sin in mortality, but also ultimately "our spirits must have become like unto [the devil], and we become devils, angels to a devil, to be shut out from the presence of our God, and to remain with the father of lies, in misery, like unto himself" (2 Nephi 9:7, 9). As Elder Boyd K. Packer testified, "I readily confess that I would find no peace, neither happiness nor safety, in a world without repentance. I do not know what I should do if there were no way for me to erase my mistakes. The agony would be more than I could bear" (*Ensign*, May 1988, 71). "O how great the goodness of our God," declared Jacob, "who prepareth a way for our escape from the grasp of this awful monster; yea, that monster, death and hell" (2 Nephi 9:10). The way has been prepared that troubled souls can be soothed and calmed. The stains of sin can be cleansed. Hope can replace despair and the tears of sinful sorrow can be wiped off our faces. Joy can swallow up guilt. "Though your sins be as scarlet, they shall be as white as snow; though they be red like crimson, they shall be as wool" (Isaiah 1:18). We need not carry life's heaviest burden any longer. The terrible price for our iniquities has already been paid for us. . . .

[The] incomprehensible suffering of the Savior was [truly] a vicarious suffering. It was *our* suffering—"inexpressible horrors"—which the Lord willingly and lovingly took upon himself in order that we might be spared such torment if we repent. Though he, of himself, was sinless and thus would not have had to experience in any degree the penalty for sin, he could not bear to let us suffer when he had the power to intercede in our behalf. Why would he willingly consent to such unfathomable and unspeakable suffering when we as mere mortals shrink from comparatively infinitesimal discomfiture? Why? Because of his infinite and incomprehensible love for us.

Guilt for Innocence

Stephen E. Robinson

Since I have on occasion given in to my temptations and Jesus never did, since I am guilty and he never was, how can he understand the sinner? How can our Savior claim to be fully human and to understand human beings if he has never experienced human sin and guilt? How can a perfect, sinless being comprehend my private agony of unworthiness? Does he know what it's like to look in a mirror and despise what he sees looking back at him? Does he know what it is to wander through the ashes of a life destroyed by one's own choices? Human beings are inevitably the arsonists of their own happiness. What can sweet, sinless Jesus possibly know about the dark side of being human?

According to the scriptures, he knows more of the dark side than any of us. In fact, he knows more about pain, grief, loneliness, contradiction, shame, rejection, betrayal, anguish, depression, and guilt than all of us combined. For in the Garden of Gethsemane and on the hill of Calvary, Jesus took upon himself the sins and the pains of all the world. "Surely he hath borne our griefs, and carried our sorrows: yet we did esteem him stricken, smitten of God, and afflicted. But he was wounded for our transgressions, he was bruised for our iniquities: the chastisement of our peace was upon him; and with his stripes we are healed" (Isaiah 53:4–5).

I would like to draw attention to a few aspects of the Savior's vicarious suffering that often escape notice, but that are important for understanding our relationship with him.

First, Jesus Christ did not just assume the *punishment* for our sins—he took the *guilt* as well. The sin, the experience itself with all of its negative consequences and ramifications, and not just the penalty for sin, became his. This is a crucial distinction. In the Atonement, Jesus does not just suffer our punishment for us, he becomes the guilty party in our place— *he becomes guilty for us and experiences our guilt:* "For he hath made him to be sin for us, who knew no sin; that we might be made the righteousness of God in him" (2 Corinthians 5:21).

In Christ there is a real transfer of guilt for innocence. Through the oneness of our covenant relationship, my guilt becomes Jesus' guilt, which he experienced and for which he suffered. At the same time, his innocence and perfection become mine, and I am rendered clean and worthy. In Christ our sins cease to be ours, and as far as the justice of God is concerned, we never committed them. Through the Atonement, we are not merely forgiven—we are rendered innocent once again. . . .

In experiencing both our punishment and our guilt, Jesus learned vicariously through the Atonement what it would have felt like to commit the sins he never committed. Thus, in a sense it would be correct to say that while Jesus committed no sins, he has been guilty of them all and knows intimately and personally their awful weight. Through us, by bearing our guilt, the sinless One experienced the full horror of human sinfulness, not merely the sins of one life, but of all lives—the sins of the world. Thus through his vicarious atonement, Jesus knows more than anyone about the dark side of being human. Even in that he is preeminent among us.

Take Him at His Word

Marion G. Romney

When a person qualifies himself to receive the blessing of this aspect of Christ's atonement [repentance], he is by the power of God forgiven of his sins; he is born again of the Spirit; he is a new person; he takes on the divine nature; he has "no more disposition to do evil, but to do good continually" (Mosiah 5:2); he has peace of conscience and is filled with joy (see Mosiah 4:3). This is what Jesus meant when He said:

"Come unto me, all ye that labour and are heavy laden, and I will give you rest.

"Take my yoke upon you, and learn of me; for I am meek and lowly in heart: and ye shall find rest unto your souls.

"For my yoke is easy, and my burden is light" (Matthew 11:28–30).

If all men would believe Jesus, take him at his word, and obey his commandments, man-made troubles and sorrows would melt away as the hoarfrost before the rising sun.

The Miracle of Change

Robert L. Millet

What mortal can snatch pride and selfishness, lust and lewdness from a natural man and create a clean heart in its place? Indeed, no man but the Man of Holiness and the Son of Man can do such things; these are works and wonders beyond the power of even the most spiritually mature Saints to do. Servants of the Lord can and do function at their Master's behest in administering the gospel to the children of men. Legal administrators—agents of the Lord—can and do represent their divine principal in leading lost souls back to the fold of the Good Shepherd. But the miracle of change, the miracle associated with the renovation and regeneration of fallen man, is the work of a God. The true Saints of God have come to know and rely upon that transcendent power.

The Greatest Miracle

Howard W. Hunter

Surely the resurrection is the center of every Christian's faith; it is the greatest of all of the miracles performed by the Savior of the world. Without it, we are indeed left hopeless. . . .

Go with me back in time to those final scenes in the Holy Land. The end of our Lord's mortal life was near. He had healed the sick, raised the dead, and expounded the scriptures, including those prophecies of his own death and resurrection. He said to his disciples:

"Behold, we go up to Jerusalem; and the Son of man shall be betrayed unto the chief priests and unto the scribes, and they shall condemn him to death,

"And shall deliver him to the Gentiles to mock, and to scourge, and to crucify him: and the third day he shall rise again" (Matthew 20:18–19). . . .

In the hours that followed, he sweat drops of blood, was scourged by the very leaders who claimed to be custodians of his law, and was crucified in the company of thieves. . . .

Think of it! When his body was taken from the cross and hastily placed in a borrowed tomb, he, the sinless Son of God, had already taken upon him not only the sins and temptations of every human soul who will repent, but all of our sickness and grief and pain of every kind. He suffered these afflictions as we suffer them, according to the flesh. He suffered them all. He did this to perfect his mercy and his ability to lift us above every earthly trial.

But there remained one more set of chains to be broken before the Atonement could be complete: the bands of death. . . .

When the women came to the tomb, they found it open and empty. The angels had tarried to tell them the greatest news ever to fall on human ears: "He is not here: for he is risen, as he said" (Matthew 28:6). . . .

In the days that followed his resurrection, the Lord appeared unto many. He displayed his five special wounds to them. He walked and talked and ate with them, as if to prove beyond a doubt that a resurrected body is indeed a physical body of tangible flesh and bones. . . .

It is the responsibility and joy of all men and women everywhere to "seek this Jesus of whom the prophets and apostles have [testified]" (Ether 12:41) and to have the spiritual witness of his divinity. It is the right and blessing of all who humbly seek, to hear the voice of the Holy Spirit, bearing witness of the Father and his resurrected Son.

As one called and ordained to bear witness of the name of Jesus Christ to all the world, I testify . . . that he lives. He has a glorified, immortal body of flesh and bones. He is the Only Begotten Son of the Father in the flesh. He is the Savior, the Light and Life of the world.

The Empty Tomb

Ezra Taft Benson

I have stood in reverent awe at the Garden Tomb in Jerusalem. It is history's most significant tomb—because it is empty!

On the third day following His burial, Jesus came forth. . . .

Of all the marks of Jesus' divinity, none has greater support by the testimony of eyewitnesses than His literal, bodily resurrection:

Several women testified that they saw Him alive.

Two disciples on the road to Emmaus dined with Him.

Peter proclaimed himself an eyewitness to the resurrection.

There were many special appearances of the risen Lord to the Twelve.

In addition to these testimonies, over five hundred saw Him at one time.

Paul certified that he saw the resurrected Lord.

Since the day of resurrection when Jesus became the "firstfruits of them that slept" (1 Corinthians 15:20), there have been those who disbelieve and scoff. . . .

I give you my testimony: The resurrection of Jesus Christ is the greatest historical event in the world to date.

He lives! He lives with a resurrected body. There is no truth nor fact of which I am more assured than the truth of the literal resurrection of our Lord.

"Don't Cry!"

David O. McKay

At some time or other every human being faces that which we call death. When I was but a boy, I sensed this deeply in the cry of a mother who sat by the side of the casket that contained her little boy. Several of us boys had been playing with firecrackers on Twenty-eighth street in Ogden. We did not know then that one of our playmates had powder in his pocket. . . . Unfortunately, in a moment of thoughtlessness, this young boy broke what we called a "lighter," and while it still had sparks in it, he put it in his pocket where the powder lay, and an explosion occurred. His clothes were set on fire, which we, his associates, tried to extinguish as best we could; but he was very severely and fatally burned.

Two or three days later his playmates sat in the funeral services. I chanced to be near enough to the mother to hear President Charles F. Middleton say: "Don't cry, Ann! Don't cry! You'll meet your boy again." And then . . . a cry came from that mother's soul in these words: "Oh, if I only knew!" That is all. I did not know its significance then. I could just respond to the cry. But since, I have read in that cry the answer to the longing of the human heart.

No parent can lay aside a child without longing, without wishing, that the child might come again, or that the parent might speak with the child again. . . . No husband can kneel at the side of a departed wife; no wife can kneel at the side of a departed husband; no child can part with a loving parent without being filled with an ardent desire to meet that loved one again somewhere in a better world where the pangs of parting are unknown. . . .

Living in posterity is not immortality . . . ; living in deeds, living in writings, living in monuments, living in the memory of friends is not immortality; neither is living in the lives of our children and our grandchildren to the latest generation . . . the immortality that Jesus had in mind when he said: "And whosoever liveth and believeth in me shall never die." (John 11:26.) . . .

To sincere believers in Christianity, to all who accept Christ as their Savior, his resurrection is not a symbolism but a reality.

As Christ lived after death, so shall all men, each taking his place in the next world for which he has best fitted himself. . . .

"He is not here: but is risen." (Luke 24:6.) Because our Redeemer lives, so shall we.

The Ultimate Triumph

Howard W. Hunter

Alexander the Great, king of Macedon, pupil of Aristotle, conqueror of most of the known world in his time, was one of the world's great young leaders. After years of exercising military pomp and prowess and after extending his kingdom from Macedonia to Egypt and from Cyprus to India, he wept when there seemed to be no more world to conquer. Then, as evidence of just how ephemeral such power is, Alexander caught a fever and died at thirty-three years of age. The vast kingdom he had gained virtually died with him.

Quite a different young leader also died at what seems such an untimely age of thirty-three. He likewise was a king, a pupil, and a conqueror. Yet he received no honors from man, achieved no territorial conquests, rose to no political station. So far as we know, he never held a sword nor wore even a single piece of armor. But the Kingdom he established still flourishes some two thousand years later. His power was not of this world.

The differences between Alexander and this equally young Nazarene are many. But the greatest difference is in their ultimate victories. Alexander conquered lands, peoples, principalities, and earthly kingdoms. But he who is called the Perfect Leader, he who was and is the Light and Life of the world—Jesus Christ the Son of God—conquered what neither Alexander nor any other could defeat or overcome: Jesus of Nazareth conquered death. Against the medals and monuments of centuries of men's fleeting victories stands the only monument necessary to mark the eternal triumph—an empty garden tomb. . . .

Without the Resurrection, the gospel of Jesus Christ becomes a litany of wise sayings and seemingly unexplainable miracles—but sayings and miracles with no ultimate triumph. No, the ultimate triumph is in the ultimate miracle: for the first time in the history of mankind, one who was dead raised himself into living immortality. He *was* the Son of God, the Son of our immortal Father in Heaven, and his triumph over physical and spiritual death is the good news every Christian tongue should speak.

The Breadth and Depth of the Gift

And he shall go forth, suffering pains and afflictions and temptations of every kind; and this that the word might be fulfilled which saith he will take upon him the pains and the sicknesses of his people. And he will take upon him death, that he may loose the bands of death which bind his people; and he will take upon him their infirmities, that his bowels may be filled with mercy, according to the flesh, that he may know according to the flesh how to succor his people according to their infirmities.

ALMA 7:11–12

Our Only Chance

S h e r i   D e w

The Lord knows the way because He *is* the way and is our only chance for successfully negotiating mortality. His Atonement makes available all of the power, peace, light, and strength that we need to deal with life's challenges—those ranging from our own mistakes and sins to trials over which we have no control but we still feel pain.

The Lord has promised to heal our broken hearts and "to set at liberty them that are bruised" (Luke 4:18); to give power to the faint, to heal the wounded soul, and to turn our weakness into strength (see Isaiah 40:29; Jacob 2:8; Ether 12:27); to take upon Him our pains and sicknesses, to blot out our transgressions if we repent, and loose the bands of death (see Alma 7:11–13). He promised that if we will build our lives upon His rock, the devil will have no power over us (see Helaman 5:12). And He has vowed that He will never leave us or forsake us (see Hebrews 13:5). There is simply no mortal equivalent. Not in terms of commitment, power, or love. He is our only chance.

Our responsibility is to learn to draw upon the power of the Atonement. Otherwise we walk through mortality relying solely on our own strength. And to do that is to invite the frustration of failure and to refuse the most resplendent gift in time or eternity. "For what doth it profit a man if a gift is bestowed . . . and he receive not the gift?" (D&C 88:33). . . . The Lord is our advocate, and He "knoweth the weakness of man and how to succor them who are tempted"

(D&C 62:1). In other words, He knows how to succor *all* of us. But *we* activate the power of the Atonement in our lives. We do this by first believing in Him, by repenting, by obeying His commandments, by partaking of sacred ordinances and keeping covenants, and by seeking after Him in fasting and prayer, in the scriptures, and in the temple. . . .

May we recommit to seek after this Jesus, of whom the prophets have testified. May we yoke ourselves to Him, draw liberally upon the matchless power of His Atonement, and rise up as sons and daughters of God and shake off the world. To "those who will have him to be their God" (1 Nephi 17:40), the Lord has extended a magnificent promise: "I will go before your face. I will be on your right hand and on your left, and my Spirit shall be in your hearts, and mine angels round about you, to bear you up" (D&C 84:88). Jesus Christ is our only chance. He will show us the way because He *is* the way.

Lifting Power

Tad R. Callister

The Atonement was designed to do more than restore us to the "starting line"—more than just wipe the slate clean. Its crowning purpose is to endow us with power so that we might overcome each of our weaknesses and acquire the divine traits that would make us like God. The Atonement was meant to be not only redemptive but exalting in its nature. C. S. Lewis understood this principle: "For God is not merely mending, not simply restoring a *status quo*. *Redeemed humanity is to be something more glorious than unfallen humanity would have been . . .*" (*Miracles,* New York, 1978, 2–3; emphasis added).

Some of us lose sight and hope of perfection and godhood, not because of major sins but because of innocent mistakes or weaknesses. "I'm not a bad person," we say. "I just can't seem to overcome the weaknesses that so easily beset me and distance me from God. It's not the sins so much as the lack of talent, the lack of capability, the lack of strength that separate me from God." Those of us who fall within this category need to be reminded of the Atonement's lifting, as well as cleansing powers. Regardless of the depth or multiplicity of our individual weaknesses, the Atonement is always there. Therein lies its beauty and genius—it is never beyond our grasp. The Savior is always standing by, anxiously longing to endow us with those powers that will convert our every weakness to a strength.

The Language of the Atonement

Bette S. Molgard

When the murky shadows of the everyday battles of life cause us to call out in the dark, the Savior will come and with him bring light. He knows our battles. He understands our fear and discouragement. His is the ultimate empathy. . . .

As we go through life we learn different "languages." A single sister doesn't feel much comfort from speaking about her situation to a mother with a home full of children. They don't speak the same language. A young mother struggling with a teething baby won't get much sympathy or any empathy from her sixteen-year-old brother. He doesn't speak her young mother language. That young mother can give sympathy to a middle-aged mother struggling with a delinquent son, but a mother who has been through the same experience actually speaks the language and can offer so much more. . . .

Our Savior felt the pain of our everyday battles in the Garden of Gethsemane. He felt every fear, discouragement, every single hurt the adversary can throw at us. I don't know how he did it. I only know that he somehow individually felt and fought every single one of my battles, and every single one of your battles. He did it so that he would know exactly how to comfort and succor us. The Atonement allowed him to understand all of our languages.

Blessings of Spiritual Renewal

Darin Cozzens

Christ's sacrifice applies to every facet of our spiritual well-being. I don't mean to oversimplify, but human beings have spirits, and those spirits are as subject to fatigue as any muscle or backbone; they are as susceptible to flagging concentration as any eye long trained on close, tedious work. There are seasons in life that gnaw and deplete our spirits just as certainly as hard work grinds at our bodies.

The most obvious detriment to our spirit is sin—of whatever magnitude. The Atonement can, on condition of our repentance, cleanse us. The miracle of the Atonement is that its effects go even beyond cleansing. President Boyd K. Packer has said, "I do not know what I should do if there were no way for me to erase my mistakes" (*Ensign*, May 1988, 71).

Just how vital is an eraser? All I know, from my own experience, is that I would no more sit down to write without some means of deleting vague, trite, or awkwardly arranged words than I would set out to build a house with a clawless hammer. Without the Atonement, our sins would forever prevent any sort of spiritual renewal. Without Jesus Christ, we truly would be lost.

From Joseph F. Smith comes a rather unsettling thought about our limitations in making things right: "Who shall repair," he asks, "the wrongs [men and women] have done to themselves and to others, which it seems impossible for them to repair themselves?" (*Gospel Doctrine*, Salt Lake City, 1977, 98).

Cleanse, erase, repair. And we can augment the list: *Heal, hearten, comfort, correct, cheer.* These are powerful verbs, and they all relate directly to the spiritual renewal effected by the Atonement. We notice, too, that most of these words apply to spiritual ailments and weaknesses beyond easily recognized and definable sin.

Even if we could fully eschew wrongdoing of every kind, eradicate all sin from our thoughts and actions, we still might make garden-variety mistakes, commit embarrassing errors and gaffes, stumble and blunder at least once in a while. In certain circumstances, we might still feel inept and inadequate and helpless. From time to time, we might still know a measure of distress or fear or regret.

Even without sin, we might choose one of two seemingly good and appealing alternatives only to realize, in retrospect, that the one passed over was indeed the better. In short, we might still make mistakes of all shades and descriptions. And as if our own mistakes and failings aren't sobering enough, we must live with the mistakes of others.

One of the eternal principles taught in the gospel is that opposition always "must needs be" (2 Nephi 2:11). But no matter what form that opposition takes, no matter its source, the Atonement extends to and strengthens us, lifts and comforts and, in reality, renews our spirits. "The blessed news of the gospel," Elder Bruce C. Hafen explains, "is that the Atonement of Jesus Christ can purify all the uncleanness and sweeten all the bitterness we taste" (*Ensign*, April 1990, 10). Whatever the source of our anxieties, whatever our level of responsibility regarding them, the Atonement's alleviating influence applies:

"Between the poles of sin and adversity . . . lie such intermediate points as unwise choices and hasty judgments. In these cases, it may be unclear just how much personal fault we bear for the bitter fruits we may taste or cause others to taste. Bitterness may taste the same, whatever its source, and it can destroy our peace, break our hearts, and separate us from God. Could it be that the great 'at-one-ment' of Christ could put back together the broken parts and give beauty to the ashes of experience such as this?" (Ibid.).

The answer, thankfully, is yes. The Atonement can do just that.

It is only the Atonement that ultimately makes life worth living, only the Atonement of Jesus Christ that can make winter-weary people feel at peace with themselves.

Living Water

Sally B. Palmer

Jesus said, . . . "In the barren deserts there shall come forth pools of living water; and the parched ground shall no longer be a thirsty land" (D&C 133:29). He said his voice shall be "as the voice of many waters, . . . which shall break down the mountains" (D&C 133:22). Jesus said, "I will give unto him that is athirst . . . of the water of life" (Revelation 21:6).

The scriptures are full of images of Christ as water and of his atonement as the water of life. For me, the Atonement is that ocean wave at the seashore that makes everything smooth again. . . .

. . . How can wrecked lives be restored; how can broken families be healed; how can destroyed bodies regain wholeness; how can wasted years be brought back; how can crushed hopes and testimonies be regained?

"Restoring what you cannot restore, healing the wound you cannot heal, fixing that which you broke and you cannot fix is the very purpose of the atonement of Christ. . . . There is no habit, no addiction, no rebellion, no transgression, no apostasy, no crime exempted from the promise of complete forgiveness. That is the promise of the atonement of Christ." That is a powerful statement from latter-day apostle Boyd K. Packer (*Ensign*, November 1995, 19–20). Think of it when you lift that tiny paper cup to your lips Sunday morning and let those few drops slide across your tongue. This is just a symbolic portion of the mighty force of the living water. Not only can it heal the unhealable but its awesome power can change the landscape in other ways, too. It has the power to crash against the rocky cliffs, sending its spray high into the air; to crush huge boulders into sand, carve valleys out of mountains, and dash ships and cities into bits.

The Atonement is infinite. The ocean is endless; the waves, constant. Eventually, every hole, every gorge will disappear without a trace, no matter how ravaged the landscape, through the atonement of Jesus Christ. To qualify for that wave of cleansing water, we have to repent of the wrongs we have done. We must acknowledge the mess we've made, be sorry for its ugliness, and try to smooth it out ourselves. We may have to live with it for a time, while the tide's out, suffering perhaps by having to put up with the gritty sand blowing about in our eyes, or the salt, or the debris that's strewn around. But eventually the wave will come, and then, like Alma, we will exclaim, "Oh, what joy . . . yea, my soul was filled with joy as exceeding as was my pain!" (Alma 36:20).

Close your eyes; see the living water run into your soul and fill up your empty spaces with peace. Feel the cool spray on your cheeks, and hear the wavelet's whisper. "Every one that thirsteth, come ye to the waters" (Isaiah 55:1) and "with joy shall ye draw water out of the wells of salvation" (Isaiah 12:3).

He Will

W. Jeffrey Marsh

[Christ's] mercy is the ultimate expression of His love for us. As Isaiah explained, He will teach us, comfort us, give us beauty, anoint us with the oil of joy, and clothe us with the garment of praise (see Isaiah 61:3). The Atonement provides eternal life, but it is also a real power that helps us throughout life. It is our immediate help as well as our eternal hope.

The indescribable suffering which caused the Savior to descend below all things was something He willingly submitted to "because of his loving kindness and his long-suffering towards the children of men" (1 Nephi 19:9). Being thus filled with mercy, He now extends that loving-kindness and long-suffering to us. . . .

He will sustain and support us.

He will warn us of impending danger.

He will enlighten us.

He will strengthen and deliver us.

He will shield us.

He will change our nature.

He will give us peace and joy.

He will encircle us in the arms of his mercy.

Beauty from Ashes

Marie Hafen

The gospel of Jesus Christ was not given us to prevent our pain. The gospel was given us to heal our pain.

That is the promise of the scriptures: the Atonement not only can heal us but it can sanctify our trying experiences to our growth. . . .

This healing, strengthening power is not a vague abstraction of distant hope. This power flows from the fully developed theology of the Atonement. Our most fundamental doctrine truly does speak to our most fundamental problems. Listen to the Lord's words from Isaiah, noting that his promises flow from his atonement: "O Israel, fear not: for I have redeemed thee, I have called thee by thy name; thou art mine. When thou passest through the waters, I will be with thee; and through the rivers, they shall not overflow thee: when thou walkest through the fire, thou shalt not be burned; neither shall the flame kindle upon thee" (Isaiah 43:1–2).

The Lord can and will sanctify our experience for our growth and development. . . . [But] the doctrine is not just that adversity can help us learn and grow; rather, it is that Christ, because of what flows from the redemption, gives us the power to make weak things strong, to sift beauty from the ashes of our fires.

For Sin and Sorrow

Gerald N. Lund

One of the things I learned as a bishop was that not all suffering and sorrow comes from transgression or violation of the laws of God. . . . I think of the newspaper account of a young mother who, as she was driving along the freeway, turned to look to a crying child in the back seat. She lost control of the car. There was a terrible accident, and lives were lost. That was not a sin. It was a mistake. But the consequences were tragic for her and for her family.

In other cases, we may face suffering and tragedy that are part of this fallen, mortal world in which we live. Some of that tragedy comes when people sin against others. The sinner is not the only one who suffers; so do the innocent. And there is also the suffering of illness, handicaps, natural disaster, and loss. . . .

. . . Here is a principle to comfort every soul. Not only did Christ suffer for our sins but he also took upon himself other things—our pains, afflictions, and temptations of every kind—and suffered for them as well (see 2 Nephi 9:21; Alma 7:11). . . .

. . . The finite human mind cannot comprehend how this is possible or what suffering the Savior took upon himself to pay the consequences not only of all the sins of the world but also all the suffering, all the sickness, all the pain, all the infirmities that mankind has suffered through thousands of years of living in a fallen world. Yet, if this were not so, then there would not be perfect justice for all. In no other way could justice ever be done.

Safe Passage

Elaine Sorensen Marshall

Grace, the divine gift of the Atonement, is a healing balm readily available to relieve our pain, a nourishing manna to assuage the hungers of our daily lives. In the arithmetic of the universe, how may grief, regret, or disappointment be accounted for when repentance does not apply or restitution is not possible? Only God's grace can balance the account. Elder Gene R. Cook taught that "Christ was sent not only to help us heal the wounds of transgression and iniquity, but also to bear our grief and sorrow and guilt" (*New Era*, December 1988, 4).

I have been haunted by countless evidences of my own negligence and inadequacies, which only Christ's atonement will redeem. I see them in the faces of my children when I disappoint them. Poor decisions may cause our families to . . . suffer; we are negligent or unconscious of acts and words that harm or destroy. The greater part of hurt, guilt, loss, and regret is borne privately, in a quiet heart, away from the warmth and casseroles of supportive friends or family. St. Exupéry wrote in *The Little Prince*, "It is such a secret place, the land of tears" (New York, 1943, 31). Grace brings to that place the gift of healing that allows peace and growth. . . .

Anyone who would be a disciple of Christ kneels sometime at Gethsemane. But . . . we need not stay. When we can find the courage to surrender, to accept the gift of the Savior—who already suffered there—we can stand and move on to another garden. Grace offers the quiet promise of that safe passage.

"My Yoke Is Easy"

Sharon G. Larsen

The gospel is intended to lighten our burden. In the gospel covenant, we are in partnership with the Savior. That is what makes his yoke easy. When we are yoked with him, Heavenly Father accepts our combined total worthiness. Christ makes his yoke easy for us, but do we believe him when he tells us that he will? Do we believe he really is who he said he is and will do for us what he said he would do? . . .

. . . When he says his yoke is easy and his burden light, he does not mean that his burden would cause no pain, no suffering, no staggering under its load, no sacrifice. In fact, it calls for the greatest sacrifice of all—our old selves, our natural selves that are an enemy to God (see Mosiah 3:19). . . .

Taking Christ's yoke upon us is the vital step we take toward godhood. We can't skip this step on the ladder. It is receiving the incomprehensibly exquisite gift of the Atonement. Elder F. Enzio Busche warned us, "We will not be satisfied until we have surrendered our lives into the arms of the loving Christ, and until He has become the doer of all our deeds and He has become the speaker of all our words" (*Ensign,* November 1993, 26).

When you decide it's Christ's yoke you want, you will quit resisting his love, and the weight of your burden will be equalized by his yoke. You will find that your half of the yoke, your own capacity, has taken an exponential leap. . . .

His yoke is easy for us, but it wasn't for him. Not at any

time in his mortal life was it easy—from his birth in a lowly stable to his cruel death on Golgotha.

His atonement was infinite. It covered everything that is not perfect from the beginning of this world to the end. His atonement was intimate because in that garden in Gethsemane, the Redeemer of the world somehow completely paid for our own personal burdens of disappointment, sin, and guilt. That's why his yoke is easy for us—and so heavy for him. He paid the awful price of justice so we could rest in mercy's arms with him forever.

He Will Never Desert Us

S h e r i   D e w

[In] my early thirties . . . I faced a personal disappointment that broke my heart. From a point of view distorted by emotional pain, I couldn't believe that anything or anyone could take away the loneliness or that I would ever feel whole or happy again. In an effort to find peace, comfort, and strength, I turned to the Lord in a way I had not before. The scriptures became a lifeline, filled as they were with promises I had never noticed in quite the same way—that he would heal my broken heart and take away my pain, that he would succor, or run to, me and deliver me from disappointment.

Fasting and prayer took on new intensity, and the temple became a place of refuge and revelation. What I learned was not only that the Lord could help me but that he would. Me. A regular, farm-grown member of the Church with no fancy titles or spectacular callings. It was during that agonizing period that I began to discover how magnificent, penetrating, and personal the power of the Atonement is.

I pleaded with the Lord to change my circumstances, because I knew I could never be happy until he did. Instead, he changed my heart. I asked him to take away my burden, but he strengthened me so that I could bear my burdens with ease (see Mosiah 24:15). I had always been a believer, but I'm not sure I had understood what, or who, it was I believed in.

President George Q. Cannon described what I experienced: "When we went forth into the waters of baptism and covenanted with our Father in Heaven to serve Him and keep His commandments, He bound Himself also by covenant to us that He would never desert us, never leave us to ourselves, never forget us, that in the midst of trials and hardships, when everything was arrayed against us, He would be near unto us and would sustain us. That was His covenant" (*Gospel Truth*, Salt Lake City, 1974, 134). . . .

Do you believe that the Savior will really do for *you* what he has said he will do? That he can ease the sting of loneliness and enable you to deal with that haunting sense of inadequacy? That he will help you forgive? That he can fill you with optimism and hope? That he will help you resist your greatest temptation and tame your most annoying weakness? That he will respond to your deepest longing? That he is the only source of comfort, strength, direction, and peace that will not change, will not betray you, and will never let you down?

An unwillingness to believe that the Savior stands ready to deliver us from our difficulties is tantamount to refusing the gift. It is tragic when we refuse to turn to him who paid the ultimate price and let him lift us up. *Life is a test.* But divine assistance is available to help us successfully complete this most critical examination.

Since that difficult period ten years ago, I have had many opportunities to experience the workings of the Lord in my life. He hasn't always given me what I've asked, and the answers haven't always come easily. But he has never left me alone, and he has never let me down.

Sure and Steady
and Supreme

Patricia T. Holland

What we too often fail to realize is that at the same time we covenant with God, *he is covenanting with us*—promising blessings, privileges, and pleasures our eyes have not yet seen and our ears have not yet heard. Though we may see our part in the matter of faithfulness going by fits and starts, by bumps and bursts, our progress erratic at best, God's part is sure and steady and supreme. We may stumble, but he never does. We may falter, but he never will. We may feel out of control, but he never is. The reason the keeping of covenants is so important to us is at least partly because it makes the contract so binding to God. Covenants forge a link between our telestial, mortal struggles and God's celestial, immortal powers.

We bring all we can to the agreement, even if that doesn't seem like much. Our heart, our devotion, our integrity—we bring as much as we can, but he brings eternity to it: he brings himself, priesthood and principalities, power and majesty beyond our wildest imagination. Just listen to the sure language of God's covenantal promise to us in 3 Nephi: "For the mountains shall depart and the hills be removed, but my kindness shall not depart from thee, neither shall the covenant of my peace be removed, saith the Lord that hath mercy on thee" (3 Nephi 22:10). God is saying, in effect, Think of the most unlikely things in the world, impossible things like the mountains departing and the hills being removed—think of the most preposterous events you can imagine, but still, even if they do, even then my kindness shall not depart from thee, neither shall the covenant of my peace be removed. . . .

The danger, of course, is that in times of pain or sorrow, times when the obedience and the sacrifice seem too great (or at least too immediate), we hesitate, we pull back from this divine relationship. How often when we have been asked to give our hearts, or give something from our heart, or give that latter-day sacrifice of a broken heart and a contrite spirit—how often when there is a difficult time or a bruising of our soul, do we shy away or openly retreat from a total and uncompromising trust in the One who knows exactly how to accept our gift and return it tenfold? God knows how to receive a broken heart, bless it, and give it back healed and renewed. He knows how to weep with love over such an offered gift, immediately bless it, mend it, and return it.

With God, whatever has become broken can be fixed. God doesn't just pull out the tiny spikes that life's tribulations have driven into us. He doesn't simply pull out what one writer has called the nails of our own guilt, leaving us bleeding and scarred forever. No, when we can finally trust our lives, our hearts, our whole souls to the Great Physician, then he not only heals what was but goes one better and makes all things new. . . . He gives us a new strength of soul, a new birth, a new heart—holier and happier, healthier than it ever was before.

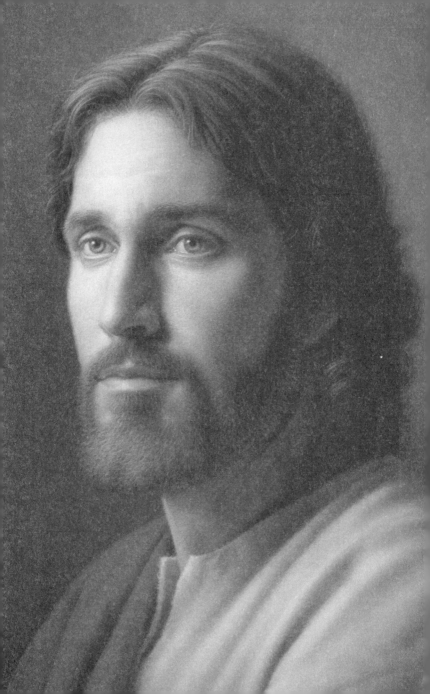

Come unto Christ

And now, . . . I would that ye should come unto Christ,

who is the Holy One of Israel, and partake of his salva-

tion, and the power of his redemption. Yea, come unto

him, and offer your whole souls as an offering unto

him, and continue in fasting and praying, and endure

to the end; and as the Lord liveth ye will be saved.

OMNI 1:26

"Oh, It Is Wonderful!"

Ezra Taft Benson

As a church, we are in accord with an ancient prophet who said, "It is by grace that we are saved, after all we can do" (2 Nephi 25:23). Grace consists of God's gift to His children wherein He gave His Only Begotten Son in order that whosoever would believe in Him and comply with His laws and ordinances would have everlasting life. . . .

By His grace and by our faith in His atonement and our repentance of our sins, we receive the strength to do the necessary works that we otherwise could not do by our own power.

By His grace, we receive an endowment of blessing and spiritual strength that may eventually lead us to eternal life if we endure to the end.

By His grace, we become more like His divine personality.

Yes, it is "by grace that we are saved, after all we can do." What is meant by the phrase "after all we can do"?

"After all we can do" includes extending our best effort.

"After all we can do" includes living His commandments.

"After all we can do" includes loving our fellowmen and praying for those who regard us as their adversary.

"After all we can do" means clothing the naked, feeding the hungry, visiting the sick, and giving "succor [to] those that stand in need of [our] succor" (Mosiah 4:16), remembering that what we do unto one of the least of God's children, we do unto Him (Matthew 25:40).

"After all we can do" means leading chaste, clean, pure lives, being scrupulously honest in all our dealings, and treating others the way we would want to be treated.

As I contemplate the glorious atonement of our Lord, which extended from Gethsemane to Golgotha, I am led to exclaim with reverence and gratitude:

I stand all amazed at the love Jesus offers me,
Confused at the grace that so fully he proffers me;
I tremble to know that for me he was crucified,
That for me, a sinner, he suffered, he bled and died.

I marvel that he would descend from his throne divine
To rescue a soul so rebellious and proud as mine;
That he should extend his great love unto such as I,
Sufficient to own, to redeem, and to justify.

Oh, it is wonderful that he should care for me,
Enough to die for me!
Oh, it is wonderful, wonderful to me! (Hymns, no. 193)

Open the Door

Chieko N. Okazaki

When I think about what I would wish for every sister in the Church, I wish for a gift so powerful that it will sustain us into the eternities, so personal that only you can understand how completely it matches who you are and what you need, so joy-producing that you will feel like shouting hallelujah. That gift is a true knowledge of our Savior, Jesus Christ. He is the light of the world. That's what will really bring light into our lives. We need to know him. Not just concepts about him. Not just lists of things he wants us to do. Not just stories from the scriptures or from other people's testimonies, but our very own stories.

Our spirituality will increase, I believe, not necessarily as we spend more time with Jesus but as we let him spend more time with us, in our daily activities. We tend to compartmentalize our lives, or divide them up, into separate little cubbyholes labeled "family," "church," "gardening," and so on. I think we sometimes have the mistaken notion that religion is like a special room in our house. We go into this room when we need to "do" religion. After all, we cook in the kitchen, we entertain in the living room, we wash in the bathroom, we sleep in the bedroom, and we "do" religion in this spiritual room. You know what's wrong with that view of the religious life? It means that we can walk out of that room and close the door behind us. It means that we have compartmentalized our lives so that religious experience is just one cubbyhole out of many. It also means that we spend most of our time in other rooms. And we feel guilty because we keep hearing that it should be the most important room in the house and we should spend most of our time there. Does this sound just the tiniest bit familiar?

Instead, perhaps we should think of our spiritual lives, not as a separate room, but as the paint on the walls of all the rooms, or maybe a scent in the air that drifts through all the rooms—the way the fragrance of spaghetti sauce or baking bread has a way of drifting through all the rooms of the house, becoming part of the very air we breathe. Our spiritual lives should *be* our lives, not just a separate compartment in our lives.

Let me put it another way: Suppose the Savior comes to visit you. You've rushed around and vacuumed the guest room, put the best sheets on the bed, even got some tulips in a vase on the dresser. Jesus looks around the room, then says, "Oh, thank you for inviting me into your home. Please tell me about your life."

You say, "I will in just a minute, but something's boiling over on the stove, and I need to let the cat out."

Jesus says, "I know a lot about cats and stoves. I'll come with you."

"Oh, no," you say. "I couldn't let you do that." And you rush out, carefully closing the door behind you.

And while you're turning down the stove, the phone rings, and then Jason comes in with a scrape on his elbow, and the visiting teacher supervisor calls for your report, and then it's suppertime, and you couldn't possibly have Jesus see that you don't even have place mats, for Pete's sake, and someone forgot to turn on the dishwasher so that you're eating off paper plates, and then you have to drive Lynne to her basketball game. So by the time you get back to the room where Jesus is still patiently waiting for you, you're so tired that you can barely keep your eyes open—let alone sit worshipfully at Jesus' feet to wait for those words of profound wisdom and spiritual power to wash over you, to make you different, to make everything else different—and you fall asleep whispering, "I'm sorry. I'll try to do better. I'm so sorry." . . .

So do you really think you're shielding him by keeping the door closed while you're throwing paper plates on the table and sending Chrissie off to wash her hands for the second time? Do you really think he doesn't know? doesn't understand? wouldn't laugh and help?

But he'll stay in that room if you put him there. Do you know why? Because if one great constant in the universe is the unfailing love of the Savior, the other great constant is his unfailing respect for human agency. He will not override your will, even for your own good. He will not compel you to accept his help. He will not force you to accept his companionship. He leaves you free to choose.

I beg you to open the door and let him out of that room. Give him your whole heart, all the pieces, and let him heal you. He promises us, "And ye shall seek me, and find me, when ye shall search for me with all your heart" (Jeremiah 29:13). "With all [our] heart[s]." That means we don't have pieces of our hearts that he doesn't touch or that aren't relevant to him. That means we must live our lives as Savior-focused individuals. Jesus doesn't call you to abandon Jason's scraped elbow when you come unto him. He calls you to bandage Jason's scraped elbow as a Savior-focused mother. Let him be with you as you bandage Jason's scrape. Let him join in the conversation over those soggy paper plates. Let him carpool with you, fill out the quarterly budget with you, attend that sales seminar with you, talk over that Young Women's lesson with your daughter, try out for the wrestling team with your son, be with your mother when the doctor tells her the diagnosis.

He's not waiting for us to be perfect. Perfect people don't need a Savior. He came to save his people in their imperfections. He is the Lord of the living, and the living make mistakes. He's not embarrassed by us, angry at us, or shocked. He wants us in our brokenness, in our unhappiness, in our guilt and our grief. . . .

We need him, and he is ready to come to us, if we'll open the door and let him.

Fools before God

Truman G. Madsen

To whom . . . will Christ not open? The scriptures tell us: those who continue to cling to denial and self-justification and become hardened in sin and neglect, those who continue to lay waste their potential, those who are imprisoned in the traditions of their fathers and who suppress the light that is "plainly manifest unto them . . . and every man whose spirit receiveth not the light is under condemnation" (D&C 93:31–32).

Christ asks that we immerse ourselves in the depths of humility and consider ourselves what we are: fools before God. We are to acknowledge that however learned or wise or experienced or talented we may be, we are, in comparison to God, mere fools and in dire need. Of those of us who, because we are "puffed up," refuse his invitation, it is said uncompromisingly, "He will not open unto them" (2 Nephi 9:42). Until we acknowledge the truth of our situation, our weakness, and our dependence, we cannot be helped. Therefore we must remain outside his fold. How long must we, like the prodigal son, eat husks until we recognize this truth for ourselves? As C. S. Lewis puts it, "If we will not learn to eat the only food that the universe grows—the only food that any possible universe ever can grow—then we must starve eternally" (*The Problem of Pain*, New York, 1962, 54).

Always Remember

Ardeth G. Kapp

When time stands still and the veil seems very thin, questions flood into our minds. "He did all of that for me, though he didn't have to? But he did! Whatever he asks of us, is it too much? Maybe it is not enough. Surely it is not enough." In the silence of our hearts, we feel a burning conviction, a personal testimony that he did that for us. And then the awesome thought, "What if, just what if, he paid that awesome price for me, to redeem me, to save me, to be my personal Savior, and that price was paid in vain in my behalf because in my daily life I choose not to do my part?"

What is our part? How do we express our gratitude? How do we always remember and never forget? It is the sacrament, the holy priesthood ordinance, that helps remind us of the Savior's atonement and our sacred covenants. It is a precious and sacred reminder, not just on Sunday, but on Monday, Tuesday, and Wednesday, spring, summer, and fall, when we are on the mountain peaks of our lives but maybe even more so in the valleys. It is often in the valleys with our afflictions that we are truly humbled and better prepared to remember the gift of eternal life for which he paid the price—those times when we feel least worthy, least comfortable about carrying his holy name, and have a keener sense of our imperfections, those moments when the flesh is weak and our spirits suffer disappointment for our errors and our sins. We might feel a sense of withdrawal, a pulling away, a feeling of needing to set aside for a time at least that divine relationship with the Savior until we are more worthy. But at that very moment, even in our unworthiness, the offer is again given to us to accept the great gift of the Atonement—even before we change. When we feel the need to pull away, let us reach out to him. Instead of feeling the need to resist, let us submit to his will. Let us bend our will as well as our knees in humble supplication.

A New Kind of Joy

George W. Pace

As you really search the scriptures and study with all your heart, you discover that there may well be a possibility that you are not as sinless as you would like to be or should be. You realize that perhaps the reason you aren't receiving more revelation and happiness in your life or fulfilling your stewardship as you should is because you don't enjoy sufficient power from the Holy Ghost.

So, like Enos, you hunger and thirst as you never have before for a complete remission of your sins. Oh, it's true you've been baptized, but you are mindful that having hands on your head and the word of promise spoken over you may not be the same thing as being baptized of the Spirit. Consistently you go to the Lord in humble prayer and plead with him that you may receive a remission of your sins.

Let me share with you a way to imagine the Atonement that might make it more real for you. Suppose that you were to review your life with the Savior, the occasions where you broke the commandments. How would you feel? Just the idea would bother me greatly, because I feel so ashamed of my sins. Imagine how that guilt would be quickened by the presence of the Savior, how painful it would be to know that the Lord has really seen all of your weaknesses and your willful disobedience. What a heartbreaking experience! Particularly when you realize that there is no way for you to make amends for your sins.

Then, perhaps, your mind goes back to the account of

the Lord in Gethsemane, of how he was so burdened with sorrow and the agony of suffering that drops of blood came from his pores. You realize that part of his suffering was to pay for your sins.

When I contemplate this, after repentance, something happens. I feel a new kind of joy and peace. I feel clean, changed. I find myself with a whole new nature (see Alma 36:20–21). I realize that this change is a result of his magnificent love and willingness to assume the pain and suffering caused by my disobedience (see Mosiah 5:2). And, oh, how I rejoice for that tremendous blessing!

Power unto Life

Truman G. Madsen

To those of us . . . who thirst, I plead, Come to him. He turns no penitent one away. Would you, if you had paid so much in suffering? Would you ever give up? All doors that are locked against the Lord are locked by us. He is always waiting, promising life where there has been death, healing where there has been sickness, forgiveness where there has been sin. And sin is poison. He sets us all an inversion of our own example. We say to people who have hurt us: "If you will change, I will forgive you—but not until. If you deserve forgiveness, you shall have it." But Christ said to the woman taken in adultery, as he wrote in the sand in the outer court of the temple (the only writing of his that is mentioned in the four Gospels), "Where are thine accusers?" You remember her reply. He said: "Neither do I condemn thee; go, and sin no more" (JST, John 8:10–11). The Joseph Smith Translation adds a sentence: "And the woman glorified God from that hour, and believed on his name." The offer of forgiveness *before* we have changed in order that we may change—that is the power of Christ. And it brings flowing, living water to the famished soul. . . .

How more could the Lord have taught us this than when he identified himself over and over with the elements of life?

"I am the living bread."

"I am the true fountain."

"He that believeth on me, as the scripture hath said, out

of his belly shall flow rivers of living water. But this [says John] spake he of the Spirit."

"I am the vine."

"Ye are the branches."

"I am the life."

"Without me ye can do nothing."

May God bless us to come hungering and thirsting and receive the birth and rebirth that is in Jesus Christ until we, like him, are "quickened in the inner man."

Captained by Christ

Ezra Taft Benson

When you choose to follow Christ, you choose to be changed. . . .

The Lord works from the inside out. The world works from the outside in. The world would take people out of the slums. Christ takes the slums out of people, and then they take themselves out of the slums. The world would mold men by changing their environment. Christ changes men, who then change their environment. The world would shape human behavior, but Christ can change human nature. . . .

Yes, Christ changes men, and changed men can change the world. Men changed for Christ will be captained by Christ. Like Paul they will be asking, "Lord, what wilt thou have me to do?" (Acts 9:6). Peter stated they will "follow his steps" (1 Peter 2:21). John said they will "walk, even as he walked" (1 John 2:6).

Finally, men captained by Christ will be consumed in Christ. To paraphrase President Harold B. Lee, they set fire in others because they are on fire (*Stand Ye in Holy Places*, Salt Lake City, 1974, 192).

Their will is swallowed up in His will (see John 5:30). They do always those things that please the Lord (see John 8:29). Not only would they die for the Lord, but more important they want to live for Him.

Enter their homes, and the pictures on their walls, the books on their shelves, the music in the air, their words and acts reveal them as Christians. They stand as witnesses of

God at all times, and in all things, and in all places (see Mosiah 18:9). They have Christ on their minds, as they look unto Him in every thought (see D&C 6:36). They have Christ in their hearts as their affections are placed on Him forever (see Alma 37:36). . . .

In Book of Mormon language, they "feast upon the words of Christ" (2 Nephi 32:3), "talk of Christ" (2 Nephi 25:26), "rejoice in Christ" (2 Nephi 25:26), "are made alive in Christ" (2 Nephi 25:25), and "glory in [their] Jesus" (see 2 Nephi 33:6). In short, they lose themselves in the Lord, and find eternal life (see Luke 17:33).

Coming to the Gift

Holy Father, keep through thine own name those

whom thou hast given me, . . . That they all may be

one; as thou, Father, art in me, and I in thee, that

they also may be one in us. . . . I in them, and thou

in me, that they may be made perfect in one; and

that the world may know that thou hast sent me,

and hast loved them, as thou hast loved me.

JOHN 17:11, 21, 23

"Love So Amazing"

Truman G. Madsen

Some time ago, the Tabernacle Choir performed in Jerusalem within the sequestered garden known as the Garden Tomb. For nearly three hours that sacred place was reserved for them to make a video recording. No place in the holy city is more evocative of events that took place during the last week in Jesus' life. Perhaps that is the . . . actual open tomb where he turned Mary's tears of sorrow into tears of joy on resurrection's morning.

In that impressive setting the choir rehearsed and sang the moving and powerful anthem, "When I Survey the Wondrous Cross," sometimes called "Love So Amazing." The song's final stanzas read:

See from his head, his hands, his feet,
Sorrow and blood flow mingled down!
Did e'er such love and sorrow meet,
Or thorns compose so rich a crown?

Were the whole realm of nature mine,
That were a present far too small;
Love, so amazing, so divine,
Demands my soul, my life, my all! . . .

We watched as members of the choir prepared, rehearsed, strolled in silence, then returned to their positions. We read in their faces increasing awe, renewal, and smothering joy. As they faced the tomb and listened to the words they themselves were singing, each "take" was more revelatory. A kind of musical covenant was being renewed in the glorious voice they gave to the melody and inspiring text. It was as if we were hearing the singing that ushered the baby Jesus into the world and that will accompany him the second time, when he returns amidst clouds of glory.

Perhaps the choir did not need the visual aid. Perhaps they brought to this hour more than they found. But it is not enough to say that the experience was impressive to those of us who stood listening nearby. The music and the words permeated all the sensitive places in our souls. . . .

We all live with the awareness that there are emotional depths within us that cannot be expressed. In the scriptures that span the ages, the prophets have dwelt with particular delight on the scene yet to come: the day of reunion, when we are encircled in the arms of Christ's love. At that great finale, our hearts will be given the wings of song as one voice:

"All shall know me, who remain, even from the least unto the greatest, . . . and shall see eye to eye, and shall lift up their voice, and with the voice together sing this new song, saying: . . . The Lord hath redeemed his people; . . . the Lord hath gathered all things in one" (D&C 84:98, 100).

This is what prophets and patriarchs have called the "new song," the song of newness, "the song of redeeming love" (D&C 84:98; Alma 5:26). In that burst of harmony, we will rejoice in the echo of Christ's high-priestly prayer: "That they all may be one; as thou, Father, art in me, and I in thee, that they also may be one in us: that the world may believe that thou has sent me" (John 17:21).

The at-one-ment of Jesus Christ achieves that all-inclusive oneness. There is no higher manifestation of love.

Pieces of Peace

Janet Lee

Christ healed bodies, minds, and souls. But after he healed the lepers, were they free from other struggles? After he restored sight to the blind, were they free from fear? Were the five thousand Christ fed ever hungry again? Was the sea calmed by Christ's hands stirred by future storms? Yes. As Helaman warned his children, the winds will continue to blow (see Helaman 5:12).

I often think of the tender last moments Christ shared with his apostles. Concerned, Christ tells his disciples that the time has come for him to leave. Full of heartache, the apostles turn to their Lord, who senses their sorrow. He replies, "Nevertheless I tell you the truth; It is expedient for you that I go away; for if I go not away, the Comforter will not come unto you; but if I depart, I will send him unto you" (John 16:7). If we expect mountains to move, seas to part, thunder to cease, and blinding light to point the way, we will miss the Savior's offering, his gift of comfort and peace. Peace comes as we truly rely on the Holy Ghost. . . .

The Lord promises safety and protection. He offers to all the gift of peace. Sometimes peace comes dramatically, like the calming of a raging sea (see Mark 4:39). Most of the time, however, peace comes quietly, as a subtle feeling of wellness, a renewed sense of God's omnipotent power, and the still, small voice whispering God's messages: words of comfort, thoughts of hope, feelings of strength, and a reassurance of love—the language of peace . . .

The Lord can speak peace to our minds wherever we are. We don't have to be in the temple or on a beautiful beach. Sometimes we are in the midst of trials and strife. It is the gift of peace that brings joy, surety, and solace—the kind of peace that can never be taken away. Piece by piece throughout a lifetime, we will long to return to the presence of the Prince of Peace. Our pieces of peace will fit together like a puzzle as our life takes shape after the pattern of our Savior. Because we are mortal, at times we will be unable to find the peace that is our gift, but our Savior's love can lift us soaring to new heights. In three short lines, Victor Hugo sings my theme song of this past year:

> Be like the bird who, halting in [her] flight on a limb too slight
> Feels it give way beneath [her],
> Yet sings knowing [she] hath wings. . . .

The boughs beneath us break sometimes. We will not fall. We have wings of truth, wings of faith, wings of glory—gifts of peace from our Savior, Master, and King.

"Can't We Ever Be Friends Again?"

Stephen E. Robinson

When my son Michael was six or seven, he did something I thought was wrong. He is my only son, and I want him to be better than his dad was. So when he slipped up, I sent him to his room with the instructions, "Don't you dare come out until I come and get you!"

And then I forgot. Some hours later, as I was watching television, I heard his door open and tentative footsteps coming down the hall. I slapped my forehead and ran to meet him. There he was with swollen eyes and tears on his cheeks. He looked up at me—not quite sure he should have come out—and said, "Dad, can't we ever be friends again?" I melted and pulled him to me. He's my boy, and I love him.

We all do things that disappoint our Father in Heaven, that separate us from his presence, his Spirit. There are times when we get sent to our rooms, spiritually though not physically. When that happens, we sometimes lift up our eyes and say, "O Father, can't we ever be friends again?" The answer, found in all the scriptures, is a resounding "Yes—through the atonement of Christ."

"Who Shall Separate Us?"

Ardeth G. Kapp

Could there ever be a time in our lives when we are striving to keep the commandments, to be obedient, yes, even to sacrifice in our small way, yet we cannot feel his arms of love and mercy? Could it ever be that he would reach out but we wouldn't let him in? He says to each of us every day of our lives, "Behold, I stand at the door, and knock: if any man hear my voice, and open the door, I will come in to him, and will sup with him, and he with me" (Revelation 3:20). Do we ever refuse to open the door, maybe because we are too busy or too tired, or because we don't hear the knock, or because we even question on occasion that he is there?

In my own life, I remember a very difficult time when I, not realizing it, refused to let him in. It was Mother's Day. At the close of the Sunday School meeting, a young woman participating in the traditional tribute to mothers tried to push a little potted geranium, not yet in bloom, into my clenched-tight fist. The clenched fist was symbolic of my heart and my mind, uptight with a myriad of unanswered questions. Why? Why?

Something about the innocence of this young girl's face softened my heart enough to at least make me open my hand and accept the gift. I took the little plant home. In time, the rays of the early morning sun released the buds, which gradually came into bloom and opened up into bright pink blossoms. From this little plant I had wanted to refuse came a message: "If you will just open your hand and your heart, the

Son, the Son of God, will come to you." I bear testimony that if—instead of wrapping our empty and aching arms around ourselves—we will open our arms, he will encircle us in his arms, his arms of mercy, his arms of love and understanding, and we will be able to open our arms to others. If through doubt and fear we clench our fists, he can't get through. . . .

You recall the account of Mary Magdalene burdened with grief as she stooped to look into the empty tomb. Her whole heart consumed by the anxiety of the moment, she did not recognize the person standing next to her. In the quiet of that garden setting, in the springtime of the year and the freshness of a new day, the Savior spoke her name: "Mary" (John 20:16). One word turned her grief to joy. She recognized his voice. She recognized him. . . .

Let us rise to the great challenge that faces us, using the words of Paul for our pledge: "Who shall separate us from the love of Christ? shall tribulation, or distress, or persecution, or famine, or nakedness, or peril, or sword? . . . Nay, in all these things we are more than conquerors through him that loved us. For I am persuaded that neither death, nor life, nor angels, nor principalities, nor powers, nor things present, nor things to come, nor height, nor depth, nor any other creature, shall be able to separate us from the love of God, which is in Christ Jesus our Lord" (Romans 8:35, 37–39).

Ask for His Help

Wendy L. Watson

The Savior entreats us to come unto him. He wants us to come close to him. He wants us to have increasingly repeated interactions with him and to really get to know him. . . .

As we increase our interactions with the Savior—as we really come unto him—we can become like him. . . . We will increase in our ability to see more like him, to love more like him, and to be more like him.

The ultimate and only true and living change agent is the Savior. He is the source of all change. He changed water into wine—bringing the very best liquid refreshment to the celebration. As you turn to him, he will bring the very best out of you. He will indeed rescue all that is finest down deep inside of you. And what a celebration that will be!

Ask for his help. Asking for the Savior's help is another way to come closer unto him.

The Savior changed eyes. And he can give you the eyes to see what you need to see in order to change your life. He will open the eyes of your understanding. Just ask for his help.

The Savior changed ears. And he can help you hear his voice, and that will add strength to your own voice. Ask for his help.

He changed limbs that were weak. And he can change your mobility and direction to help you move to the next level of your life and help you in your efforts to shore up the feeble knees that are around you. Ask for his help.

He changed a few fishes and a couple of loaves of bread into enough to feed 5,000 people. And he will take your widow's mite of time, energy, and ability and magnify them, multiply them, so that there is enough and to spare. You just need to ask for his help.

The Savior changed names: he turned Saul into Paul. And he can help you become his son or daughter. You can thus take upon you his name in a whole new way.

Although our Lord Jesus Christ never changes, he is the quintessential change agent—the only true change agent. Don't you love that seeming irony: the only true change agent never changes! There is only one true and living change agent—and he changes not. And he loves you. And he loves your desire and your efforts to change.

His desire is for you to change, to have a change of heart, a change of nature, and to, over time, completely cast off the natural man. He did all that he did so that you could change! He is your Savior and my Savior!

We need to actively, persistently plead for the power of his infinite and atoning sacrifice to be applied in our lives. And as we do so, his ultimate healing will bring to each of our lives the ultimate change.

The Divine Embrace

Hugh Nibley

People are usually surprised to learn that *atonement,* an accepted theological term, is neither from a Greek nor a Latin word, but is good old English and really does mean, when we write it out, at-*one*-ment, denoting both a state of being "at one" with another and the process by which that end is achieved. The word *atonement* appears only once in the New Testament (Romans 5:11) in the King James Version, and in the Revised Standard Version it does not appear at all, since the new translation prefers the more familiar word "reconciliation." Paul has just told us that the Lord "sat down at the right hand of the Majesty on High," so reconciliation is a very good word for atonement there, since it means literally to be seated again with someone (*re-con-silio*)—so that atonement is to be reunited with God. . . .

Most interesting is the Arabic *kafata,* . . . as it is the key to a dramatic situation.

It was the custom for one fleeing for his life in the desert to seek protection in the tent of a great sheik, crying out, "*Ana dakhiluka,*" meaning "I am thy suppliant," whereupon the lord would place the hem of his robe over the guest's shoulder and declare him under his protection. In the Book of Mormon, we see this world as a plain, a dark and dreary waste, a desert. We see Nephi fleeing from an evil thing that is pursuing him. In great danger, he prays the Lord to give him an open road in the low way, to block his pursuers, and to make them stumble. He comes to the tent of the Lord and enters as a suppliant; and in reply, the Master, as was the ancient custom, puts the hem of his robe protectively over the kneeling man's shoulder *(kafata)*. This puts him under the Lord's protection from all enemies. They embrace in a close hug, as Arab chiefs still do; the Lord makes a place for him and invites him to sit down beside him—they are at-*one* (2 Nephi 4:33; Alma 5:24).

This is the imagery of the Atonement, the embrace: "The Lord hath redeemed my soul from hell; I have beheld his glory, and I am encircled about eternally in the arms of his love" (2 Nephi 1:15). "O Lord, wilt thou encircle me around in the robe of thy righteousness! O Lord, wilt thou make a way for mine escape before mine enemies!" (2 Nephi 4:33). "Behold, he sendeth an invitation unto all men, for the arms of mercy are extended towards them, and he saith: Repent, and I will receive you" (Alma 5:33).

"In His Arms"

Tad R. Callister

This reconciliation between God and man is figuratively and literally symbolized by an embrace. Lehi alluded to this in his dying sermon to his sons: "The Lord hath redeemed my soul from hell; I have beheld his glory, and I am encircled about eternally in the arms of his love" (2 Nephi 1:15). The Doctrine and Covenants suggests the same imagery: "Be faithful and diligent in keeping the commandments of God, and I will encircle thee in the arms of my love" (D&C 6:20). Amulek preached in like fashion: "Mercy can satisfy the demands of justice, and encircles them in the arms of safety" (Alma 34:16). What a beautiful metaphor. What child does not feel safety in the arms of his kind and loving father? What peace, what warmth, what reassurance, to know that in his arms he is safe from crime, anger, rejection, loneliness, and all the ills of this world.

Isaiah spoke of those tender moments when the Lord would "gather the lambs with his arm, and carry them in his bosom" (Isaiah 40:11). Elder Orson F. Whitney experienced such a glorious moment when he saw a marvelous manifestation of the Savior. In his dream, he said, "I ran [to meet Him] . . . , fell at his feet, clasped Him around the knees, and begged Him to take me with Him. I shall never forget the kind and gentle manner in which He stooped, raised me up, *and embraced me.* It was so vivid, so real. I felt the very warmth of His body, as He held me in His arms" (*Through*

Memory's Halls, Independence, Missouri, 1930, 83; emphasis added). Who would not long for that warmth, that embrace?

Who among us will be safely encircled in those arms of love? Are there a chosen few reserved for this honor? Alma lets it be known there is no exclusionary policy: "Behold, he sendeth an invitation unto all men, for the arms of mercy are extended towards them" (Alma 5:33; see also 2 Nephi 26:25–33). That is what the Savior told the Nephites at the time of his appearance: "Behold, mine arm of mercy is extended towards you, and whosoever will come, him will I receive" (3 Nephi 9:14). . . .

Contemplate for a moment the magnetic pull when a little child sees her father on bended knee with arms extended. The invitation is irresistible. The reaction to return is automatic. There is no intellectual analysis. It is like reaching for a blanket in cold weather, turning on the light in a dark room. Some things are not mind-driven, but heart-prompted. These are natural yearnings of the soul— the need for warmth, light, and love. Likewise, our Father in Heaven is extending his arms with the intent to entice us home. How irresistible those arms are to those who seek his warmth, his light, and his love. He invites us to the day of reconciliation, the return to our true home, the day of reunification with our primeval family; he invites us to run to his arms and bask in his embrace. This was the Lord's promise to the children of Israel: "I will redeem you with a stretched out arm. . . . And I will take you to me for a people, and I will be to you a God" (Exodus 6:6–7).

He Spoke My Name

Melvin J. Ballard

Away on the Fort Peck Reservation where I was doing missionary work with some of our brethren, . . . I found myself one evening in the dreams of the night in that sacred building, the temple. After a season of prayer and rejoicing I was informed that I should have the privilege of entering into one of those rooms, to meet a glorious Personage, and, as I entered the door, I saw, seated on a raised platform, the most glorious Being my eyes have ever beheld or that I ever conceived existed in all the eternal worlds. As I approached to be introduced, he arose and stepped towards me with extended arms, and he smiled as he softly spoke my name. If I shall live to be a million years old, I shall never forget that smile. He took me into his arms and kissed me, pressed me to his bosom, and blessed me, until the marrow of my bones seemed to melt! When he had finished, I fell at his feet, and, as I bathed them with my tears and kisses, I saw the prints of the nails in the feet of the Redeemer of the world. The feeling that I had in the presence of him who hath all things in his hands, to have his love, his affection, and his blessing was such that if I ever can receive that of which I had but a foretaste, I would give all that I am, all that I ever hope to be, to feel what I then felt! . . .

I see Jesus not now upon the cross. I do not see his brow pierced with thorns nor his hands torn with the nails, but I see him smiling, with extended arms, saying to us all: "Come unto me!"

Sources

Our Deepest Need

"The Means of Escape" by Joseph Fielding Smith, from "Salvation Universal," *Improvement Era*, 13 (December 1909): 145–46.

"Paying the Debt" by Melvin J. Ballard, from *Sermons and Missionary Services of Melvin Joseph Ballard*, compiled by Bryant S. Hinckley (Salt Lake City: Deseret Book Co., 1949), 167, 169–70.

"The Parable of the Bicycle" by Stephen E. Robinson, from "Believing Christ," *Ensign*, April 1992, 8–9.

"An Empty Sacrament Table" by Tad R. Callister, from *The Infinite Atonement* (Salt Lake City: Deseret Book Co., 2000), 54–55.

"Our Desperate Needs" by Truman G. Madsen, from "The Suffering Servant," in *The Redeemer: Reflections on the Life and Teachings of Jesus Christ* (Salt Lake City: Deseret Book Co., 2000), 227–28.

The Greatest Descent

"A God Is Born" by Bruce R. McConkie, from "A God Is Born," in *Christmas Classics: A Treasury for Latter-day Saints* (Salt Lake City: Deseret Book, 1995), 10, 14–16.

"Divine Payment, Divine Peace" by J. Reuben Clark Jr., from *Behold the Lamb of God* (Salt Lake City: Deseret Book Co., 1991), 120–21.

"The Servant King" by Truman G. Madsen, from "The Suffering Servant," in *The Redeemer: Reflections on the Life and Teachings of Jesus Christ* (Salt Lake City: Deseret Book Co., 2000), 229–31.

"Son of Man, Son of God" by John Taylor, from *The Mediation and Atonement* (Salt Lake City: Deseret News Co., 1882), 151.

"The Downward Journey" by Tad R. Callister, from *The Infinite Atonement* (Salt Lake City: Deseret Book Co., 2000), 96–97.

"The How and the Why" by Ezra Taft Benson, from "Jesus Christ—Our Savior and Redeemer," *Ensign,* June 1990, 4–5.

His Sacrifice in Suffering

"He Goes His Way Alone" by Spencer W. Kimball, from "Jesus of Nazareth," *Ensign,* December 1984, 2, 5–7.

"Wounded, Bruised . . ." by Bruce R. McConkie, from *A New Witness for the Articles of Faith* (Salt Lake City: Deseret Book Co., 1985), xii–xiv.

"The Olive Press" by W. Jeffrey Marsh, from *His Final Hours* (Salt Lake City: Deseret Book Co., 2000), 42–43.

"A Vision of Gethsemane" by Orson F. Whitney, from *Through Memory's Halls: The Life Story of Orson F. Whitney* (Independence, Missouri: Press of Zion's Printing and Publishing Co., 1930), 81–83.

"'And It Was Night'" by Truman G. Madsen, from *The Radiant Life* (Salt Lake City: Bookcraft, 1994), 15–17.

"The Supreme Prayer" by Bruce R. McConkie, from "Why the Lord Ordained Prayer," *Ensign,* January 1976, 7.

"A Cry from the Heart" by John Taylor, from *The Mediation and Atonement* (Salt Lake City: Deseret News Co., 1882), 149–51.

"The Statistics of Sin" by Gerald N. Lund, from *Selected Writings of Gerald N. Lund* (Salt Lake City: Deseret Book Co., 1999), 164–65.

"'An Incomprehensible Tidal Wave'" by Tad R. Callister, from *The Infinite Atonement* (Salt Lake City: Deseret Book Co., 2000), 134.

"Crossing the Line to Infinite" by Stephen E. Robinson, from *Believing Christ: The Parable of the Bicycle and Other Good News* (Salt Lake City: Deseret Book Co., 1992), 121–23.

"Victorious Christ" by James E. Talmage, from *Jesus the Christ* (Salt Lake City: Deseret Book Co., 1983), 568–69.

"The Rescue Mission" by Tad R. Callister, from *The Infinite Atonement* (Salt Lake City: Deseret Book Co., 2000), 129–31.

"No Spot of Weakness" by Gerald N. Lund, from "I Have a Question," *Ensign*, July 1975, 31.

God's Transcendent Gift

"The Cost" by Melvin J. Ballard, from *Sermons and Missionary Services of Melvin Joseph Ballard*, compiled by Bryant S. Hinckley (Salt Lake City: Deseret Book Co., 1949), 152–55.

"Merciful Love" by Gerald N. Lund, from "Salvation: By Grace or by Works?" *Ensign*, April 1981, 21–22.

"One of the Grand Constants in Nature" by Hugh Nibley, from *Approaching Zion*, edited by Don E. Norton (Salt Lake City and Provo: Deseret Book Co. and FARMS, 1989), 603.

"Once or Twice in a Thousand Years" by Bruce R. McConkie, from "Once or Twice in a Thousand Years," *Ensign*, November 1975, 15.

"The Very Heart" by George W. Pace, from *Our Search to Know the Lord* (Salt Lake City: Deseret Book Co., 1988), 75–76.

"The Work of a God" by Robert L. Millet, from *Jesus Christ: The Only Sure Foundation* (Salt Lake City: Bookcraft, 1999), 157–58.

"This I Know" by Bruce R. McConkie, from *A New Witness for the Articles of Faith* (Salt Lake City: Deseret Book Co., 1985), xvi.

An Atonement for Sin and Death

"Spiritual Estrangement" by Brent L. Top, from *Forgiveness: Christ's Priceless Gift* (Salt Lake City: Bookcraft, 1989, 1996), 3, 5–11.

"Guilt for Innocence" by Stephen E. Robinson, from *Believing Christ: The Parable of the Bicycle and Other Good News* (Salt Lake City: Deseret Book Co., 1992), 116–18.

"Take Him at His Word" by Marion G. Romney, from "Christ's Atonement: The Gift Supreme," *Ensign*, December 1973, 2.

"The Miracle of Change" by Robert L. Millet, from *Jesus Christ: The Only Sure Foundation* (Salt Lake City: Bookcraft, 1999), 94.

"The Greatest Miracle" by Howard W. Hunter, from "He Is Risen," *Ensign*, May 1988, 16–17.

"The Empty Tomb" by Ezra Taft Benson, from *Come unto Christ* (Salt Lake City: Deseret Book Co., 1983), 9–10.

"'Don't Cry!'" by David O. McKay, from "Easter—and the Meaning of Immortality" *Improvement Era* 58 (April 1955): 221.

"The Ultimate Triumph" by Howard W. Hunter, from "An Apostle's Witness of the Resurrection," *Ensign*, May 1986, 15–16.

The Breadth and Depth of the Gift

"Our Only Chance" by Sheri Dew, from "Our Only Chance," *Ensign*, May 1999, 67.

"Lifting Power" by Tad R. Callister, from "How Can I Lead a More Saintly Life?" in *Arise and Shine Forth: Talks from the 2000 Women's Conference* (Salt Lake City: Deseret Book Co., 2001), 89–90.

"The Language of the Atonement" by Bette S. Molgard, from *Everyday Battles* (Salt Lake City: Bookcraft, 1999), 11–12.

"Blessings of Spiritual Renewal" by Darin Cozzens, adapted from "The Power of Renewal," *Ensign*, April 1993, 8–9.

"Living Water" by Sally B. Palmer, from "The Atonement: A Sea of Peace," in *Clothed with Charity: Talks from the 1996 Women's Conference,* edited by Dawn Hall Anderson and others (Salt Lake City: Deseret Book Co., 1997), 118–19, 122–23.

"He Will" by W. Jeffrey Marsh, from "Remember How Merciful the Lord Hath Been," *Ensign*, April 2000, 20–25.

"Beauty from Ashes" by Marie Hafen, from "Eve Heard All These Things and Was Glad," in *Women in the Covenant of Grace: Talks Selected from the 1993 Women's Conference,* edited by Dawn Hall Anderson and Susette Fletcher Green (Salt Lake City: Deseret Book Co., 1994), 27–28.

"For Sin and Sorrow" by Gerald N. Lund, from "The Savior and Modern Revelation," in *The Redeemer: Reflections on the Life and Teachings of Jesus Christ* (Salt Lake City: Deseret Book Co., 2000), 322–23, 325–26.

"Safe Passage" by Elaine Sorensen Marshall, from "Evening Balm and Morning Manna: Daily Gifts of Healing Grace," in *Women in the Covenant of Grace: Talks Selected from the 1993 Women's Conference*, edited by Dawn Hall Anderson and Susette Fletcher Green (Salt Lake City: Deseret Book Co., 1994), 265–67.

"'My Yoke Is Easy'" by Sharon G. Larsen, from "That Summer Home in Babylon," in *The Arms of His Love: Talks from the 1999 Women's Conference* (Salt Lake City: Deseret Book Co., 2000), 24–26.

"He Will Never Desert Us" by Sheri Dew, from "This Is a Test. It Is Only a Test," in *May Christ Lift Thee Up: Talks from the 1998 Women's Conference* (Salt Lake City: Deseret Book Co., 1999), 192–93.

"Sure and Steady and Supreme" by Patricia T. Holland, from "God's Covenant of Peace," in *The Arms of His Love: Talks from the 1999 Women's Conference* (Salt Lake City: Deseret Book Co., 2000), 372–73.

Come unto Christ

"'Oh, It Is Wonderful!'" by Ezra Taft Benson, from *Come unto Christ* (Salt Lake City: Deseret Book Co., 1983), 7–9.

"Open the Door" by Chieko N. Okazaki, from "Lighten Up," in *Women and Christ—Living the Abundant Life: Talks Selected from the 1992 Women's Conference*, edited by Dawn Hall Anderson and others (Salt Lake City: Deseret Book Co., 1993), 5–8.

"Fools before God" by Truman G. Madsen, from "The Suffering Servant," in *The Redeemer: Reflections on the Life and Teachings of Jesus Christ* (Salt Lake City: Deseret Book Co., 2000), 239–40.

"Always Remember" by Ardeth G. Kapp, from *The Joy of the Journey* (Salt Lake City: Deseret Book Co., 1992), 79–80.

"A New Kind of Joy" by George W. Pace, from "What It Means to Know Christ," *Ensign*, September 1974, 47.

"Power unto Life" by Truman G. Madsen, from *The Highest in Us* (Salt Lake City: Bookcraft, 1978), 30–31.

"Captained by Christ" by Ezra Taft Benson, from *A Witness and a Warning: A Modern-day Prophet Testifies of the Book of Mormon* (Salt Lake City: Deseret Book Co., 1988), 61–62, 64–65.

Coming to the Gift

"'Love So Amazing'" by Truman G. Madsen, from "The Suffering Servant," in *The Redeemer: Reflections on the Life and Teachings of Jesus Christ* (Salt Lake City: Deseret Book Co., 2000), 245–47.

"Pieces of Peace" by Janet Lee, from "Pieces of Peace," in *Every Good Thing: Talks from the 1997 BYU Women's Conference*, edited by Dawn Hall Anderson and others (Salt Lake City: Deseret Book Co., 1998), 10–12.

"'Can't We Ever Be Friends Again?'" by Stephen E. Robinson, from "Believing Christ," *Ensign*, April 1992, 6.

"'Who Shall Separate Us?'" by Ardeth G. Kapp, from "In Mercy's Arms," in *The Arms of His Love: Talks from the 1999 Women's Conference* (Salt Lake City: Deseret Book Co., 2000), 11–13, 16.

"Ask for His Help" by Wendy L. Watson, from "Change: It's Always a Possibility," in *BYU Speeches*, 7 April 1998, 218–20.

"The Divine Embrace" by Hugh Nibley, from *Approaching Zion*, edited by Don E. Norton (Salt Lake City and Provo: Deseret Book Co. and FARMS, 1989), 556, 559.

"'In His Arms'" by Tad R. Callister, from *The Infinite Atonement* (Salt Lake City: Deseret Book Co., 2000), 27–29.

"He Spoke My Name" by Melvin J. Ballard, from *Sermons and Missionary Services of Melvin Joseph Ballard*, compiled by Bryant S. Hinckley (Salt Lake City: Deseret Book Co., 1949), 157.